NATIVE EXPERIENCE MARKETING

Praise for
NATIVE EXPERIENCE MARKETING

The best global brands are moving away from monocultural marketing to embrace *Native Experience Marketing* instead.

> —***Nataly Kelly**, Author of* Take Your Company Global *and former HubSpot VP International*

As an international business consultant, I'm continuously impressed by marketing frameworks that put the customer at the center. *Native Experience* (NX) *Marketing* does just that by emphasizing cultural insights and authentic engagement with diverse audiences. Rather than taking a one-size-fits-all approach, NX acknowledges the importance of nuanced, inclusive communication that resonates across languages and cultures. This mindset shift is exactly what global organizations need to build trust and loyalty with customers worldwide. I appreciate that NX recognizes that effective marketing is not about you but about deeply understanding buyer perspectives. This customer-centric approach is the future of marketing in our interconnected world.

> —***Renato Beninatto**, Author of* The General Theory of the Translation Company *and Nimdzi Insights Chairman and Co-Founder*

Mark's concept of NATIVE is so beautifully natural, but at the same time so missed today in our fast-paced and standardized way of interacting with each other. To turn messaging into communication, you need to acknowledge, appreciate and respect your audience. In *Native Experience Marketing*, Mark shows us how we can all take it to yet another level, turning communication into building authentic relationships by appreciating everyone's native lived experience.

> —***Andrzej Nedoma**, CEO of Nedoma.io Business Advisory and co-founder of XTRF Translation Management Systems*

In my over 20 years in the language industry, I have seen many approaches to global communication and marketing. *Native Experience Marketing* offers a fresh, insightful, and highly practical perspective that is essential for anyone looking to navigate the complex but rewarding world of intercultural business and communication. It is a testament to the power of language and culture in shaping local and global interactions and a guidebook for building more inclusive, effective, and successful in-language communication strategies.

—Josef Kubovský, CEO at Nimdzi Insights and
former Chief Evangelist at MemSource

Mark brings a refreshing perspective to marketing with this book. It is a much-needed resource for those engaged in communications, demonstrating that one size does not fit all. NX Marketing shows that it is time to move away from old and outdated stereotypes when labelling consumers or audiences who do not fit the so-called mainstream. It is a must-read for any marketing expert with its engaging writing style.

—A/Professor Erika Gonzalez, RMIT University,
Translating and Interpreting

NATIVE

HOW TO AUTHENTICALLY REACH, INCLUDE AND ENGAGE

EXPERIENCE

YOUR AUDIENCES IN *THEIR* NATIVE LANGUAGE AND CULTURE

MARKETING

MARK SABA

 First published in 2024 by LEXIGO BOOKS, an imprint of
LEXIGO Global Pty Ltd
nx@lexigo.com | +61 3 8630 2930 | lexigo.com/nx

© 2024. Mark Saba. All rights reserved.
The moral rights of the author have been asserted.

 A catalogue record for this book is available from the National Library of Australia.

Printed book ISBN: 978-0-6459997-0-9
Ebook ISBN: 978-0-6459997-1-6

All rights reserved, except as permitted under The Australian Copyright Act 1968. Apart from any fair dealing for the purposes of study, research, criticism or review, no part of this publication may be reproduced, stored or transmitted in any form or by any means, electronic, mechanical, photocopying, recording, scanning, or otherwise without written permission from the publisher. It is illegal to copy this book, post it to a website, or distribute it by any other means without permission.

This publication may contain references to external or third-party internet websites. The author and publisher have no control over and assume no responsibility for the content, privacy policies, or practices of any third-party websites. The inclusion of any URLs does not imply endorsement by the author or publisher. The accuracy, relevance, timeliness, or completeness of any information on these external websites is not guaranteed. URLs and website contents are subject to change, become outdated, or may become unavailable at any time. Readers are advised to verify any information obtained from external sources.

Designations used by companies to distinguish their products are often claimed as trademarks. All brand names and product names used in this book and on its cover are trade names, service marks, trademarks and registered trademarks of their respective owners. The publishers and the book are not associated with any product or vendor mentioned in this book. None of the companies referenced within the book have endorsed the book.

This publication is intended for general informational purposes only and does not constitute advice. The views and opinions expressed in this book are those of the author and do not necessarily reflect the official policy or position of any other agency, organisation, employer or company. The content is provided 'as is' without warranty of any kind, either express or implied, including but not limited to the implied warranties of merchantability, fitness for a particular purpose, or non-infringement. Readers should not act upon the information provided in this book without seeking professional counsel. The author and publisher are not responsible for any specific business or financial decisions made or actions taken in reliance upon the information provided herein.

LEXIGO® NX® and Be Native® ARE REGISTERED TRADEMARKS OF LEXIGO GLOBAL PTY LTD. ALL RIGHTS RESERVED WORLDWIDE.

Cultural and Linguistic Sensitivity Note

This book presents LEXIGO's proprietary framework: Native Experience Marketing or NX®. The book employs certain generalisations as a means to introduce and explain complex cultural and linguistic concepts. These generalisations are intended as starting points for discussion and understanding rather than definitive representations of diverse cultures and languages.

We recognise that each language and culture possesses its own rich and distinctive array of nuances, which broad generalisations cannot fully capture or represent. Consequently, while this book provides a foundational overview, it is important for readers to approach cultural and linguistic matters with a mindset of continuous learning and individual inquiry.

We advise against the use of generalisations as a substitute for specific, nuanced understanding in professional and personal interactions. Instead, we encourage readers to seek deeper knowledge and understanding of the specific cultural and linguistic contexts they encounter. Your feedback and insights are greatly valued and will contribute to the ongoing refinement and accuracy of our work in representing the cultural and linguistic diversity of the world we live in.

For Jamila, Isaac, Elise and Seth

Contents

Preface	*xiii*
Introduction	*xvii*
Chapter 1: THINK, DESIGN and GO Native	*1*
PHASE I: THINK	**22**
Chapter 2: Be Notable	25
Chapter 3: Be Authentic	55
PHASE II: DESIGN	**84**
Chapter 4: Be Trusted	87
Chapter 5: Be Inclusive	123
PHASE III: GO	**152**
Chapter 6: Be Versatile	155
Chapter 7: Be Evolving	179
Be NATIVE	*207*
Work with Me	*213*
Acknowledgments	*217*
Index	*221*
About the Author	*229*
About LEXIGO	*233*
About NX	*235*

Preface

FOR THE ALMOST TWENTY years I've been in the language industry, one concept has bugged me persistently. I'd find myself thinking about it at random times: while exercising, lying awake at 3:00 AM, showering, driving, or looking at ads.

Something that seemed so obvious to me just wasn't translating in the real world: What's ethnic and foreign to you is native to someone else.

Yet we constantly refer to marketing outside the 'mainstream' as 'ethnic', 'foreign' or 'multicultural'. Why aren't we considering the native experiences of these audiences? Why aren't we approaching our translation, marketing and communication efforts from a native-first—that is, *audience-first*—perspective? Even worse, why are we treating these audiences as an afterthought by simply translating English content and then being dumbfounded when we don't get the results?

It was an itch I had to scratch.

As the founder and CEO of LEXIGO, I have witnessed the undeniable impact of culturally intelligent marketing. *Native Experience Marketing (NX)* is the culmination of years of research, brainstorming and practical application. It's my answer to that thought that kept nagging at me and a blueprint for marketing strategies that truly resonate—strategies that are *NATIVE*: *Notable, Authentic, Trusted, Inclusive, Versatile* and *Evolving*.

This book is a journey through the heart of what it means to connect with audiences on a level that goes beyond the simple translation of words. It is about understanding the deep cultural characteristics and context that influence how people perceive the world around them. From the streets of London, where campaigns like Nike's 'Nothing Beats a Londoner' capture the city's vibrant spirit, to the fewer than 1,000 Iraqi Turkmens making up one of the target markets in a national health campaign, NX is about exploring native experiences to allow campaigns to generate more inclusion and understanding amongst communities and audiences.

NX Marketing is a testament to the power of cultural empathy and competency. It is a guide for building trust and rapport with audiences whose cultural nuances are as diverse as their languages. Through three phases—THINK, DESIGN and GO—this book lays out a roadmap for creating campaigns that are seen, heard, felt and remembered.

As you read, you will encounter the principles of NX; you will learn the importance of a considered NX approach, the role of diverse teams, collaboratively creating campaigns with the very audiences you aim to engage, and the significance of continuous evolution in the face of an ever-changing cultural landscape.

I invite you to start by shifting your perspective. Whether you are a marketing or communications professional, a business leader, or simply someone who believes in the power of communicating natively, NX offers a new lens through which to view the world of what you were probably taught to refer to as 'ethnic', 'foreign' or 'multicultural' marketing. It is a call to action to embrace audiences in their native language and culture, not as a challenge but as an opportunity to create a lasting impact and legacy.

Join me as we change the face of modern marketing and communication, one native experience at a time.

Introduction

DID YOU KNOW THAT there are more than 7,100 unique languages in the world? Picture this: our planet is home to a staggering 8 billion-plus people, and that number is growing every day. Each one of us contributes to a symphony of billions of words spoken in countless dialects, variations and languages.

Sure, English might be the most widely spoken language, with almost 19% of the global population using it, but here's a fun fact: roughly two-thirds of those English speakers learned it as their second language. Isn't that something?

And it doesn't stop there. Even in countries where English is the primary language, the linguistic diversity is mind-blowing. Australia? More than 200 languages. Canada? More than 190. The United Kingdom? More than 300. And the United States? A whopping 350+ languages! (And these figures don't even include Indigenous languages.)

So, as we dive into this book, let's take a moment to celebrate this incredible linguistic and cultural diversity and explore how it shapes the way we communicate and connect with each other.

Language	No. of speakers	No. of native speakers	% of world speakers
English	1.452 billion	372.9 million	18.38%
Mandarin	1.118 billion	929 million	14.15%
Hindi	602 million	343.9 million	7.62%
Spanish	548 million	474.7 million	6.94%
French	280 million	79.9 million	3.54%
Arabic	274 million	362 million*	3.47%
Bengali	272.7 million	233.7 million	3.45%
Russian	258.2 million	154 million	3.27%
Portuguese	257.7 million	232.4 million	3.26%
Urdu	231.3 million	70.2 million	2.93%

*The number of speakers and native speakers of Arabic is complex to determine. Modern Standard Arabic—the varietal used to determine the number of speakers—is a standard variety used in formal contexts across the Arab world, but it's not typically spoken as a first language. Instead, people speak various local dialects of Arabic as their native language, which puts the number of native speakers at a higher figure.

There are billions of people speaking billions of words in thousands of languages every single day. Each language represents a unique culture, and within each culture, subcultures, each with its own distinct way of thinking. It's a beautiful mosaic of human expression.

Yet we continue to label communication aimed at audiences outside the 'mainstream' as 'ethnic', 'foreign' or 'multicultural'. Doesn't that feel a bit off? Imagine being called 'foreign' in your own homeland.

Not only does this approach feel exclusionary, but it's also a misstep in marketing. By doing so, at best, we're inadvertently shrinking our potential audience, but also, more critically, damaging our reputation through disrespectful communication.

In the public sector, moreover, the need for inclusive and respectful communication is a matter of reputation and a fundamental requirement to providing access and equity to communication and services: one of the essential civil rights of a democratic society.

Governments are tasked with reaching a diverse populace, each member of which has their own linguistic and cultural context. Here, the stakes are even higher, as failing to communicate effectively doesn't only risk losing an audience, but negatively impacting the well-being and informed participation of citizens.

Let's dive deeper into this and explore a more inclusive approach.

Marketing Language Matters

'Ethnic marketing', 'foreign marketing' and 'multicultural marketing' are outdated concepts. They say more about the speaker's point of view than about the audience itself. They are terms used to describe differences that belong to a far more fractured world before the digital age and the era of globalisation. Now that we're living in a world that's more connected than ever before, the time has come to shelve those terms and leave them to gather dust.

If we want to tap into these new markets, we don't only need to change how we approach language. We need to change how we consider the audiences. Words like 'ethnic', 'foreign' and 'multicultural' bunch local audiences into a single monocultural group, when they are actually a bustling mix of many audiences and cultures.

In other words, they're human!

In today's environment, marketers are challenged to dig deeper and consider other factors. To consider factors that might not be immediately obvious. So, let me ask you this: have you ever thought about taking into account the following factors?

Factor	What to Consider	What to Do
Country	Local efforts vs international efforts.	Adjust strategies for local vs global audiences, consider cultural norms and legal regulations.
Language Proficiency	Local populations' English level vs Native language spoken at home.	Use appropriate language complexity, ensure communications are culturally sensitive at the very least.

Factor	What to Consider	What to Do
Native Thinking	Even if fluent in English, individuals may think and feel in their native language and culture.	Craft messages that resonate with the cultural mindset and emotional context.
Linguistic Nuance	Understanding native language subtleties and sub-cultures with different linguistic preferences.	Tailor content to reflect local idioms, sayings and cultural expressions.
Dialects	Variations within the primary language.	Use dialect-specific language for authenticity and better engagement.
Colour Perception	Cultural significance of colours. Safe and appealing colour choices for messages.	Select colours that align with cultural meanings and aesthetic preferences.
Communication Style	Preferred modes of communication (verbal, written, visual, gestures etc.).	Adapt communication channels and styles to audience preferences.
Generational Focus	Understanding generational differences in language and cultural assimilation.	Differentiate messaging to connect with the values and media habits of each generation.
Accessibility	Ensuring that your content is easily accessible and understandable to people with disabilities.	Incorporate features like subtitles, alt text for images and easy-to-read formats. Design your content to be compatible with screen readers and other assistive technologies.

Believe it or not, we've only just scratched the surface. There's a whole world of considerations waiting to be explored, and we're going to dive into all of it as we journey through the rest of this book.

> **Author's note:** *I struggled with the choice of using an 's' or 'z' in the word 'globalisation', and whether to spell 'colour' the British way or the American way. I was torn between staying true to my Australian-English and making sure I didn't alienate international readers. In the end, I decided to stick with what's familiar to me. As you'll discover in this book, sometimes the best choice in your communication efforts is to be authentic, even if it means tweaking your style a little.*

Bring the Conversation Forward with Native Experiences

The alternative to 'ethnic', 'foreign', and 'multicultural' marketing is Native Experience Marketing, or NX for short.

By native, I mean authentic communication that truly resonates with and respects the audience's culture. Imagine a campaign that speaks the language of each audience, regardless of their culture, heritage or language—with a native lens.

NX aims to speak through that lens, so campaigns are set up for success right from the get-go. NX is all about authentic engagement, acknowledging that non-English-speaking audiences are not one big, homogenous group.

And by 'native', I also mean actively working with people from the communities you aim to serve. These are the people who will ensure messages come across natively and authentically.

This native approach is built into a marketing campaign or initiative from the very beginning, prioritising the consideration of how to authentically communicate with each audience segment natively, not adding it as an afterthought. Before any campaign work is done—writing messaging, picking colours, designing graphics—it seeks to understand all the cultures a marketing campaign or initiative wants to reach.

NX, done correctly, can significantly boost your positioning among your target audience.

To put it simply, employing NX in your next campaign or initiative will not only gain more ground with your audience, but it might also start to earn you lifelong loyalty.

Cultural Insight: The Heart of NX

Take a page out of the book of giants like Nike. A corporate giant that understands a crucial aspect of global business: the substantial gap between their overarching corporate culture and the local nuances of their various regional markets. Nike's strategy isn't about forcing uniformity; rather, they embrace the diversity of each market. They establish local offices, staffed with marketing experts who possess an in-depth understanding of each region's unique cultural landscape, offering invaluable native insights.

Similarly, Starbucks' journey in Australia serves as a learning curve. Their initial expansion efforts, rigidly adhering to their international model without adapting to the local context, resulted in a significant setback, leading to the closure of over 250 stores across Australia. However, their subsequent attempt was marked by a strategic collaboration with local partners. This move, infusing Australian sensibilities into an American brand, paved the way for a triumphant expansion of the franchise.

So, how can your organisation replicate such success and avoid pitfalls? This is where NX comes into play. The book is crafted for government and communication professionals, enterprise teams, business owners, and marketers. Its purpose? To transform the way you perceive and engage with new audiences. By adopting a 'native lens', this book will help you shift your mindset, enabling you to reach, include, engage and grow within new markets authentically. Embrace the lessons from local and global brands and learn how to apply them in your context, ensuring a deeper and more genuine connection with your target audience.

It may be that you're already familiar with the needs of these audiences, or that you're comfortable with the concepts of localisation and hyper-localisation in marketing. What this book provides is a framework that will provide another useful tool to enable you to develop an approach that gets the most from these aspects of marketing.

At the book's heart is the NATIVE acronym, which also serves as our values at LEXIGO, the translation and native communication agency I have been running since I founded it in 2011.

It's a simple to remember yet flexible marketing framework that outlines how professionals can make their in-language, in-culture marketing and communication initiatives:

- *Notable* to the efforts as a whole
- *Authentic* in your messaging
- *Trusted* by the audiences
- *Inclusive* in approach
- *Versatile* in execution
- *Evolving* with the changing dynamics of the campaign and its audiences.

NOTABLE
AUTHENTIC
TRUSTED
INCLUSIVE
VERSATILE
EVOLVING

It is a strategy that is not static but dynamic, allowing marketing and communication teams to pivot and adapt as the cultural conversations and market conditions shift.

Introducing NX will also allow us to:

- **Identify opportunities** to reach new markets and audiences in their native language and culture—whether they are local or global. By leveraging NX, organisations can pinpoint untapped market segments that respond more favourably to culturally resonant messaging. This approach broadens the scope of potential audiences and fosters a sense of familiarity and trust among new audience demographics.
- **Present the business case to interested stakeholders**, illustrating the tangible benefits of a culturally nuanced approach. By articulating the potential for increased market share, enhanced brand loyalty and improved customer satisfaction, NX can demonstrate its value as an indispensable component of an organisation's growth strategy.
- **Develop novel ideas** to support the establishment of a genuine connection with these audiences. Creativity infused with cultural insights can lead to innovative campaigns

and initiatives that resonate on a deeper level. This may involve incorporating local idioms, customs, beliefs or values into marketing strategies, ensuring that communication is not just translated but truly transformed and created in-language to align with the cultural context.

- **Consider the many facets of NX audiences** in relation to the product and campaign. Understanding these elements is crucial for tailoring messages that capture attention and generate meaningful engagement. It requires a multifaceted analysis of demographic data, migration patterns, generational factors, cultural norms, language preferences and societal trends.

- **Engage with relevant communities and groups** that can provide authentic insights and champion an organisation's efforts. This is about finding an audience and building a community around the initiative and the brand. It involves listening to the voices within these groups, involving them in the conversation, and creating a feedback loop that ensures the messages are culturally relevant, respectful and responsive.

- **Build trust and rapport** through consistent engagement and cultivate long-term relationships with audiences through a thoughtful and sustained engagement approach. The NX approach isn't about quick wins. It's about playing the long game, nurturing relationships with your audience that stand the test of time. It's about keeping the conversation going, tweaking your engagement strategies to keep pace with your audience's evolving needs and preferences. Do this right and you'll have a loyal fan base that feels seen, heard and valued.

- **Enhance brand relevance and relatability** through native content and initiatives that speak your audience's language, and I don't just mean linguistically. It's about tailoring your content to fit the cultural landscape of each market, adapting your brand messages to resonate with local customs, beliefs, and trends. It's about being seen and, more importantly, relevant and relatable. And when your content hits home in this way, its impact and effectiveness go through the roof.

NX is a tried and tested framework, but it is not rigid or prescriptive. NX Marketing is too varied for a one-size-fits-all strategy, so this is less a specific formula than a set of guidelines. Importantly, it's not a recipe for simply attempting to mimic the culture of a specific audience. Instead, it invites audiences and relevant stakeholders in the process of developing a Native Experience, ensuring that the approach is genuinely tailored and resonant.

NX is neither exhaustive or exclusive. Depending on the situation—the size of the business, the size of the campaign, and an organisation's resources—there are dozens, if not hundreds, of other possible approaches. In addition, the method is not about international selling or marketing. It is about setting up campaigns and initiatives for success by communicating natively from the outset to all target audiences. I'm not going to share specific cultural knowledge, other than as examples to explain my points.

NX adopts a familiar structure to conventional marketing approaches, yet it distinguishes itself by placing in-language audiences at the forefront of its strategy. The essence of marketing—understanding and engaging with one's audience—is universal. However, NX refines this principle through the prism of language and cultural nuance, ensuring that the approach is audience-first, culturally-conscious, inclusive and authentic.

At the very least, NX encourages the consideration of all factors that could potentially affect a campaign's success and illustrates the many paths to explore. But the magic is where it champions the heart of marketing—building genuine, lasting relationships with communities.

This approach compels organisations to consider all factors influencing a campaign's success, paving numerous pathways for exploration. More importantly, it recognises the unique ways different audiences connect with your brand or message. This isn't just about tapping into untapped markets; it's about fostering a deep, empathetic understanding of those you serve.

Such an approach gives you a competitive advantage over those who haven't embraced this level of engagement and cements your role as a business that truly listens, understands and values its in-language markets.

It's about creating connections that endure, turning audiences into communities and transactions into relationships.

CHAPTER 1

THINK, DESIGN and GO NATIVE

*'A brand is no longer what we tell the consumer.
It's what consumers tell each other it is.'*
—SCOTT COOK, *co-founder, Intuit*

LET ME TAKE YOU back to the early days of the COVID-19 pandemic. The myriad of terms floating around added to the uncertainty and confusion already caused by the virus. Remember how it felt hearing about this new, mysterious illness for the first time? I remember, for example, how we casually referred to it as 'Corona' in the early days, often humorously clinking Corona beer bottles together—a bit of irony that I'm sure presented a unique branding challenge for Corona at the time!

Now, imagine the uncertainty of naming and comprehension multiplied by the challenge of language barriers. This was a real hurdle in Australia and across the world, especially for those who had just arrived or were still connected to their native countries' news and media cycles. For them, the Australian way of referring to the pandemic might have sounded completely wrong. That meant that any communications about the virus weren't just about the virus; they also had to make sense of it in a language the audience understood.

Our mission was to bring clarity and consistency in COVID-19 communication across 63 different languages with the Australian government.

You read that right—63 languages!

Ensuring everyone was on the same page wasn't just a matter of public health; it was about making people feel included, understood and safe in a new health environment. We set out with a clear goal: to ensure that every translated term matched the official Australian guidelines and resonated with each community's linguistic and cultural nuances. This sometimes meant the terms had to be changed or developed with communities.

It was a massive undertaking. Picture a team of native translators, cultural experts and community members all collaborating to find that perfect balance between accuracy and cultural sensitivity. And let me tell you, the feeling of getting it right was immensely gratifying.

The outcome? We managed to create a unified, clear understanding of COVID-19 across a multitude of languages and cultures. It was more than just an act of translation; it was about building trust, eliminating fear, and bringing communities together during one of the most challenging times we've faced as a nation (or, indeed, as a planet).

The experience was a powerful reminder of something I've always believed in: effective communication goes beyond words. It's about making connections, understanding differences and creating a sense of belonging, regardless of language barriers.

NX reimagines the audience-first perspective of marketing by moving beyond the audience as the starting point to delve deeper into the linguistic and cultural context in which the audience exists.

While traditional marketing approaches prioritise understanding consumer behaviour and preferences, NX enhances this by emphasising the Native Experience. This means crafting marketing communications that are audience-first and intrinsically tailored to the unique cultural and linguistic nuances that define the audience's identity. It's an approach that does more than recognise the audience—it celebrates and respects their cultural and language diversity as central to the marketing process.

It guides professionals and marketers through in-language and in-culture marketing campaign efforts to ensure they *THINK, DESIGN* and *GO* to market natively while also providing flexibility and openness to think deeper. It's impossible to cover every complexity in a single book, but the method is a jumping-off point that will help open perspective to create a truly Native Experience for your target audience that resonates and respects them, no matter the language or culture.

The beauty of culture is its diversity—but that also means that a single communication formula is not going to be effective for everyone. There is no universal formula that works for every audience, which is exactly where NX Marketing can help. NX is not intended to be a rigid, one-size-fits-all approach. Instead, NX is all about flexibility and adaptability. It allows you to create communication strategies that are as diverse and vibrant as the cultures you are reaching out to.

Beyond Monocultural Marketing

Gone are the days when advertising was solely shaped by a company's culture, branding strategies and the dominant culture or country associated with the brand. In today's world, where word of mouth is a pivotal sales metric, the consumer sits at the heart of marketing dynamics. Customers place high value on the opinions within their inner circles about a brand. A disconnect does not go unnoticed, such as a brand that champions diversity but lacks cultural representation within its ranks. Customers are quick to spot such inconsistencies and are likely to share these observations within their networks.

The challenge lies in avoiding a monocultural approach to communication, particularly when aiming to engage audiences in their native language and culture. What resonates with one segment—maybe a preference for animated, interactive media—might not hit the mark with another group that leans towards concise, analytical content.

This highlights the need for a nuanced strategy that ensures that every individual feels understood and engaged in a manner that aligns with their cultural context and communicative preferences.

Such cultural awareness of target audiences is crucial to THINK, DESIGN and GO native. That's why NX includes like-minded people in the campaign. If the aim is to authentically reach, include, engage and grow native audiences, who better to do that than someone who understands the culture natively?

Our aim is to approach these audiences with respect and awareness of their culture, customs and languages. It's about communicating in ways that resonate with them, reaching out through their preferred channels and mediums.

NX Marketing helps meet this challenge. It is broken up into three phases, each with two stages:

Phase	Stage	Focus
Think	Be Notable	Learn, Prepare, Assemble NX Teams
	Be Authentic	Research, Listen, Discover
Design	Be Trusted	Strategy, Scope, Build
	Be Inclusive	Create, Design, Test
GO	Be Versatile	Plan, Launch, Adapt
	Be Evolving	Track, Measure, Improve

Let's start with a summary of each of the chapters that make up the NX Marketing framework. For each chapter, I've also included a reflective question or prompt intended to help you measure your readiness to embrace and apply NX principles within your in-language and in-culture marketing and communication endeavours. The prompts will prepare you to fully engage with the nuanced insights and tailored advice in each part of the book.

> *For each question, score yourself from 1 to 10,* ***1 being low readiness*** *and* ***10 being high readiness***. *It's important to be honest with yourself because it's only by acknowledging where you're starting from that you can measure your progress.*

This book is structured to make it possible to hop

from one section to another as you see fit or to progress in a linear way from start to finish. Depending on your self-assessment outcomes, you may discover that your level of preparedness propels you to leap ahead, or you might prefer to measure your growth against the benchmarks provided. Whichever path you choose, this book will be a guide to enrich your understanding and refine your approach at every step of the NX journey.

> ***Author's note:*** *As you read through this book, I encourage you to make it your own by using a pencil (or pen!) to jot down notes, highlight sections and mark ideas that inspire you. This book is a practical tool, so interact with it and make it your own. The insights and strategies are designed to be applied and revisited, so by annotating and highlighting the material, you'll make it easier to apply to your professional challenges. Your notes will serve as milestones on your journey of growth. Imagine looking back and seeing how much you've evolved—evolving being one of the key ideas of this book and the ethos at LEXIGO. This book can be a living record of your growing understanding of in-language communications. Scribble, underline, highlight and reflect!*

Part I: *THINK* NATIVE

Be Notable

Reflect on a recent marketing campaign you conducted that was targeted at in-language audiences. To what extent did you consider including cultural experts?

(1) (2) (3) (4) (5) (6) (7) (8) (9) (10)

Crafting a culturally resonant and considered campaign might seem like a daunting task, but it's not impossible. This chapter sheds light on the path to creating campaigns that receive praise for their positive qualities—i.e. for their notability. These campaigns should be admired for their cultural sensitivity, authenticity and deep engagement with the audience. The idea is to tap into the untapped potential of your communication efforts. Use the diversity of thought as a catalyst for creativity, innovation and overall success.

Notability is achieved not by imitating but by integrating the voices and insights of the audience into the heart of the campaign, ensuring that every message is a true product of the community it aims to reach. Rather than superficially adapting a mainstream campaign, this alignment is about developing original content directly from these communities, reflecting their true voice and experiences.

Achieving Notability is an essential element of successful NX Marketing. It refers to the idea that the campaign's message resonates so powerfully with audiences because it is crafted through a genuine partnership that reflects and embodies the audience's cultural beliefs and values.

Such campaigns are created by representative teams with the knowledge and power of native experiences. They are distinguished by their ability to speak not only to the audience but also from within it.

This approach marks the start of a truly *Notable* journey in your NX endeavours, where the audience isn't just a receiver of the message but an integral part of its creation.

Be Authentic

Rate your confidence in distinguishing between genuine cultural expression and stereotyping in your campaigns.

(1) (2) (3) (4) (5) (6) (7) (8) (9) (10)

This stage asks how the campaign will be *Authentic* in its communication, delivery and goals. For many communities and audiences, their experience is the most critical factor in how they see a brand.

When communication is authentic and native, price and product almost become irrelevant because consumers care more about the connection they have to the brand.

Luxury brands create excellent customer experiences. Their wild success is evidence that their target markets see them as authentic. This authenticity, however, is communicated differently, depending on the market.

In the world of luxury commerce, China is an example of a thriving market for upscale brands in a culture where societal structures are deeply hierarchical and status significantly influences consumer behaviours. In these regions, more affluent consumers often seek an experience that mirrors their social stature when shopping at high-end establishments like Louis Vuitton, Prada, or Rolex. The expectation of an elevated, almost regal customer service experience is anticipated, with marketing campaigns meticulously designed to echo the sentiment of exclusivity and distinction.

In stark contrast, Australia's luxury market operates under a different cultural characteristic, largely thanks to 'Tall Poppy Syndrome'—a phenomenon discouraging overt displays of superiority or pretentiousness. For the most part, consumers here frequenting luxury boutiques prioritise subtlety and equality in service. They favour a shopping experience that emphasises the product's inherent value over a polished service, which aligns with a broader cultural preference for modesty and fair treatment across society.

This contradiction between markets serves as a globalised illustration of how deeply rooted cultural values shape consumer expectations and marketing strategies. At a local level, consider the ramifications of these cultural norms. For instance, a localised campaign in China might involve personalised outreach, exclusive events and tailored services that reinforce the brand's status and the consumer's aspirational lifestyle. Meanwhile, in Australia, localised initiatives might focus on community engagement, brand authenticity and craftsmanship stories that resonate with a preference for quality and authenticity over prestige.

Let me just mention that I'm aware that these examples are generalisations—the very thing this chapter is advising us against. In this case, however, these broad examples are designed to help ease you into the complex world of cultural nuances in marketing. As we're just starting to explore this topic, ask yourself whether you fit within the broad audience perspectives I've outlined. If not, how does that make you feel? Reflecting on this can be a useful reminder of the importance of avoiding assumptions and recognising the diverse range of experiences within any given culture.

Let's dig even deeper and imagine the nuanced approaches required at the grassroots level, where cultural intricacies can significantly impact the efficacy of a marketing campaign. While broad strategies provide direction, countries like China or Australia are not culturally homogenous but are composed of many different subcultures and individual experiences: real success lies in the ability to adapt and apply these insights in a way that feels native to each unique cultural group.

Authenticity forms the backbone of trust. It requires marketers to deliver genuine and resonant messages that are culturally adapted and rooted. Authenticity in communication fosters trust and establishes credibility.

Part II: *DESIGN* NATIVE

Be Trusted

How well do you employ strategies to build and maintain trust with your audiences?

① ② ③ ④ ⑤ ⑥ ⑦ ⑧ ⑨ ⑩

In the next chapter, we delve into an important ingredient of any lasting relationship: trust. We explore how to cultivate trust in an NX landscape and build our NX strategy through careful use of *trust signals*.

We'll discuss how trust is not one-size-fits-all; it must be carefully crafted to fit the cultural and social norms of each specific market. In order to build trust into our strategy, we can use a variety of tactics, including engaging with our audiences through social media, creating personalised email campaigns, hosting events and sponsorships, launching informative podcasts, and creating compelling content marketing. We carefully select and adapt each tactic to resonate with the unique nuances of each market, ensuring that the trust we establish is deep and long-lasting.

This stage is about laying the foundations of a strategy where trust is not an afterthought but a guiding principle at the core of every action and decision.

At this stage, we ask professionals and marketers to put themselves in their audience's shoes. The goal is to ensure communication and engagement are genuine and curated, at least in part, by people who understand the native cultures and customs of local audiences.

Navigating the landscape of language presents a formidable challenge in cultivating trust, particularly as lexicons expand and adapt to current events. The COVID-19 pandemic serves as a prime case study in the rapid evolution of language, with terminologies emerging almost overnight to facilitate clear communication. For authorities and businesses, staying abreast of these linguistic shifts was crucial to maintaining their credibility.

Be Inclusive

Rate how well your current strategies are including native audiences in your campaign development.

① ② ③ ④ ⑤ ⑥ ⑦ ⑧ ⑨ ⑩

This chapter explores the importance of inclusivity by revealing LEXIGO's approach to co-creation—a contemporary method for creating in-language, in-culture content with audiences and communities, not just for them.

As we'll see, inclusivity goes beyond representation; it's about actively collaborating with communities to ensure that our NX strategies are theoretically sound, practically effective, and culturally resonant.

Co-creation brings inclusivity to the forefront, fostering a sense of ownership among community members. It's a transformative approach that values community intelligence, authentic representation, and innovation. It's about creating a collaborative environment in which contributors are acknowledged and rewarded. It's about ideation, drafting, refining and testing creative assets through community validation.

In any form of marketing, inclusivity is a must-have. It's a powerful tool for innovation, a catalyst for authentic engagement and a pathway to long-term brand loyalty. By co-creating with communities, we ensure our marketing efforts are as diverse and dynamic as the cultures we aim to engage.

Author's note: *If you're new to the concept of co-creation, it refers to an inclusive, in-language and in-culture collaborative process in which ideas, content and strategies are developed jointly by multiple stakeholders. This concept extends beyond traditional creation methods by actively involving diverse participants in the creative process: customers, experts, community members, and other stakeholders.*

This approach means that content is crafted from scratch in-language rather than translated, so it's more effective at capturing authentic cultural nuances.

Co-creation is grounded in the principle that the collective wisdom and diversity of individuals can lead to more innovative, effective and inclusive outcomes. It doesn't seek feedback on preformed ideas; it is a blank slate that can integrate NX perspectives and expertise from the outset to shape the direction, content and execution of a project.

Co-creation ensures that our NX Marketing strategies and communications are built for and by the audience, fostering authenticity and resonance. It seeks to break down the barriers between 'creator' and 'audience', fostering a more democratic and participatory process that enhances the quality and relevance of the outcomes while building stronger connections and a sense of ownership among all those involved.

Part III: *GO NATIVE*

Be Versatile
How would you rate your brand's ability to adapt quickly to changing cultural trends and market dynamics?

(1) (2) (3) (4) (5) (6) (7) (8) (9) (10)

Launching is a critical phase of any campaign—but it's not as simple as pressing 'Go'. We need to be prepared and agile enough to deploy campaigns across different channels while measuring their outcomes in real time.

This chapter is about planning your NX launch and launching. It offers a comprehensive toolkit for readers to learn how to use grassroots distribution and other hands-on approaches effectively. It also provides insightful strategies for selecting the best media mix, allocating resources for maximum efficiency, and establishing feedback loops through KPIs—and reminds us that our strategies may need to adapt in the face of market trends, global disruptions and social movements.

Be Evolving
Rate your success in evolving with live market's cultural and sentiment shifts.

(1) (2) (3) (4) (5) (6) (7) (8) (9) (10)

The final stage in our NX journey shifts our focus to the critical post-launch period of a campaign, which requires meticulous attention to tracking and measuring long-term impact.

This chapter explores the continuous cycle of monitoring, analysis and refinement to recognise that the true measure of a campaign's success is an ever-changing target influenced by external and environmental factors. You will find the tools to stay vigilant and interpret data as numbers and narratives that reveal your NX performance in real contexts.

We'll look at how to gather feedback effectively, conduct research and redesign strategies in response to the voices of your target communities and audiences. A live campaign is a living entity that must be nurtured, understood and occasionally redirected. You will learn to evolve to meet new challenges and opportunities, ensuring that your campaigns remain relevant and resonant in the marketplace—and helping to prepare you for your next NX journey.

The first step of the method, *Notable*, is up next, but before we move on, don't forget to add up your scores to see where you stand on the NX readiness scale.

0–20: Beginning the Journey
You are at the early stages of your NX journey. There is considerable room for growth in understanding and applying NX principles effectively. Focus on PHASE I: THINK (CHAPTERS 2 and 3, BE NOTABLE and BE AUTHENTIC), which will lay the groundwork for your journey ahead.

21–30: Emerging Explorer
You've made some inroads, but there's more to discover. Delve into PHASE II: DESIGN (CHAPTERS 4 and 5, BE TRUSTED and BE INCLUSIVE) to build on your trust and inclusivity in NX markets.

31–40: Skilled Traveller
You have a solid foundation and are well-prepared to polish your skills. Delving deeper into CHAPTERS 4 and 5, BE TRUSTED and BE INCLUSIVE, in PHASE II: DESIGN will allow you to explore its concepts in more detail, enhancing your agility and proficiency in your approach.

41–50: Cultural Connoisseur

You show a high level of cultural intelligence and marketing savviness. To fine-tune your strategy, revisit CHAPTERS 6 and 7, BE VERSATILE and BE EVOLVING, in PHASE III: GO, which will help you maintain and evolve your cultural edge.

51–60: NX Navigator

Congratulations, you are a NX Navigator! Your scores reflect a strong capability and readiness in NX Marketing. Still, there's always more to learn. Use the book and its online resources to deepen your knowledge and stay ahead of the curve.

Recap

NX puts the in-language audience first in marketing communication.

- ▶ It's a framework, not a prescriptive set of rules, so it's flexible enough to adapt to complex and changing situations.
- ▶ Consumers are at the heart of modern marketing, so word-of-mouth has become a critical metric to consider.
- ▶ NX is divided into three phases: THINK, DESIGN and GO.
- ▶ THINK relates to how to create a campaign that is both Notable and Authentic.
- ▶ DESIGN is about shaping a campaign that will become Trusted and Inclusive in a complex, intercultural world, balancing a business brand with the cultures of individual societies.
- ▶ GO explores how to ensure a campaign remains *Versatile* and *Evolves* after launch through the effective analysis of results in the short, medium, and long term.

PHASE I:
THINK

WELCOME TO PHASE I: THINK. This is where you'll get equipped with the necessary knowledge, team, tools and tactics to form the building blocks of the NX framework.

IN CHAPTER 2: BE NOTABLE, I'll show you the ingredients needed to make your NX stand out and leave a lasting impression on your target audience, as well as set the benchmark for NX implementation and results in your organisation. We'll cover:

> **Knowledge:** You'll learn about the fundamental concepts, best practices and latest trends used in NX Marketing, giving you a solid foundation to work from.
>
> **Team:** You'll discover how to build a business case and assemble a diverse and inclusive team that represents your target audience with the skills and commitment needed to succeed.

We'll delve deeper into the tools and tactics in CHAPTER 3: BE AUTHENTIC to get you started on preparing your campaign for PHASE II: DESIGN.

> **Tools:** You'll be introduced to the latest tools that can help you design and implement a successful NX campaign and learn how to choose the right tools for your needs.

> **Tactics:** You'll gain practical insights into how to create engaging, relevant and memorable experiences that meet your target audience's needs and expectations.

CHAPTER 2

Be Notable

'Diversity is the engine of invention. It generates creativity that enriches the world.'
—JUSTIN TRUDEAU, *Prime Minister of Canada*

IN 2009, HSBC, THE UK-based 'world's private bank', launched a global marketing campaign based on its call to arms, 'Assume Nothing'. Soon afterwards, it was forced to launch a hasty $10 million rebranding campaign when it turned out that in a number of countries, the direct translation of the phrase was 'Do Nothing'—the diametrical opposite of its dynamic intent.

And spare a thought for US brewer Coors, which tried to promote its beer in new markets with the energising slogan 'Turn It Loose'. Only after the campaign had failed did they learn that in colloquial Spanish the phrase referred to diarrhoea.

There are countless examples of campaigns being

sabotaged by unexpected linguistic complications. One I've heard often is about General Motors' launch of the Chevy Nova in South America, where 'no va' means 'it won't go'—but I've learned when researching this book that it's actually apocryphal. But it's too good a story to leave out just because it's not true. All these examples underline the same point; creating a marketing campaign that straddles different cultures is a minefield with hidden dangers at every turn. Yet the idea of a campaign that can carry the same message equally effectively to multiple cultural groups remains a Holy Grail of marketing.

Because when it works, the results are worth the hassle.

Notable or Notorious

Creating a successful marketing campaign in a single culture can be difficult enough. Creating one that will work in more than one culture without becoming notable for all the wrong reasons is exponentially harder. What might seem like the smallest cultural misunderstandings can soon balloon from slight hiccups in a marketing strategy into notorious missteps that can lead to significant brand damage and financial loss.

There are so many potential pitfalls in understanding

and respecting cultural nuances that the whole endeavour can seem overwhelming.

What this book will show you, however, is how you can create a campaign that is notable for its positives, not its negatives. A campaign that is celebrated for its sensitivity, authenticity and engagement. A campaign that unlocks the potential of your diverse customer base.

A notable campaign harnesses the power of diverse thinking to drive creativity, innovation and success to provide a Native Experience (NX) to your audiences. By NX, I mean a campaign that speaks as powerfully to them as if it had been developed within their own cultural background, wherever they are from, because it was developed by them.

That sort of Notable campaign relies on using strategies to build and nurture diverse teams and leveraging the power of *Cultural Intelligence (CQ)*.

We'll go into that later in the chapter. First, however, a quick detour to suburban Melbourne in the 1990s and the soundtrack of my youth. There is a point, I promise. And it's not just the chance to namecheck Vanilla Ice.

HARNESS THE POWER OF DIVERSE THINKING TO DRIVE CREATIVITY

I.C.E, I.C.E Baby

When I was growing up in suburban Melbourne, playing Vanilla Ice on repeat on a Sony Walkman, I had no idea how its rich cultural diversity would impact my life, both personally and professionally. It seemed that the whole world lived in Melbourne.

For a start, there was us, the Sabas, a young Coptic Egyptian family and an example of a culture within a culture. We touched down from Egypt in 1987, when I was four and my sister was two, little knowing that we'd eventually permanently swap the Land of the Pharaohs for the Land Down Under, Australia.

My first friend in Australia was Russian. Although we couldn't communicate that well through language, we bonded over our love of chess—a universal form of communication that transcends linguistic division. My friend across the street was Greek, and there was an Argentinian bakery eight doors down from our house. At school, my classroom was like a United Nations, with kids from all sorts of cultural backgrounds, including Irish, English, Chinese, German, Vietnamese, Italian, Indian, Macedonian and others.

The same story was being repeated in schools throughout the suburbs of Melbourne. We got to experience a world of cultures without ever leaving the neighbourhood. Schools were set up so everyone got to enjoy each other's cultural celebrations, together with 'World Food Days' and 'Multicultural Day'.

We were lucky enough—most of us, anyway—to grow up with a highly developed CQ. Not everyone has a high CQ. Many people were brought up in far more monocultural societies than we were. Others rejected opportunities to learn about other cultures for various reasons.

The good news is that you can improve your CQ because it's at the foundation of NX marketing. I've created the I.C.E acronym to help leaders and teams improve their CQ by providing a crash course on cultural awareness.

Before we start, we can use the I.C.E model to get ourselves into the right headspace and positive mindset by drawing on three popular concepts to help rebaseline our CQ—the cultural:

- *Iceberg*
- *Competency*
- *Empathy*

Iceberg

The *Cultural Iceberg* is a helpful metaphor to introduce the complex nature of culture because it reminds us that while we can experience culture at a surface-level with things such as language, customs and traditions—there are also underlying values, beliefs and assumptions that shape how we think and act.

The tip of the iceberg represents the aspects of culture that are easy to observe and identify. In contrast, the submerged portion represents the invisible aspects often hidden beneath the surface. As with a real iceberg, this hidden part is far, far larger than the part we can see.

The idea of the Cultural Iceberg helps us appreciate that human cultures come in all shapes and sizes and recognise that there is much more to any culture than what meets the eye. It also helps us understand that culture is not static. Like an iceberg shaped by the ocean, culture constantly evolves as societies adapt to new situations and experiences.

Competency

We'll look more closely at the Cultural Iceberg in the next chapter, but it's an essential first part in navigating the challenges that can arise when communicating across cultures.

It's only by understanding the 90 per cent of a culture or its intrinsic aspects that are hidden beneath the surface that we can gain *Cultural Competency*, which is the next element in laying the foundation for providing a successful NX to your audiences.

Here are seven tips you or your team can take right now to start improving your Cultural Competency:

Tip 1. Increase self-awareness: Start by examining your own cultural background, biases and assumptions. Take some time to reflect on how these factors might influence your interactions with people from different cultures.

Tip 2. Learn about different cultures: Educate yourself about different cultures, particularly those you are likely to come across as part of your NX target audience. Learn about their customs, beliefs and practices. This can be done by reading, through online platforms such as TikTok, and by attending workshops and community events. Above all, it comes with interacting widely with people from diverse cultural backgrounds.

Tip 3. Challenge stereotypes and biases: Be aware of stereotypes and biases that may influence your perceptions of people from different cultures. Because these stereotypes and biases have a shallow basis, they often refer to the 10 per cent at the tip of the Cultural Iceberg. Challenge these stereotypes and biases by seeking out accurate information and perspectives.

Tip 4. Be open to feedback and willing to make mistakes: Recognise that Cultural Competency is a lifelong learning process and be open to feedback and willing to make mistakes as you continue to learn.

Tip 5. Practise active listening and effective communication: Developing effective communication skills, particularly active listening—paying attention to what people actually mean rather than to what they say—is crucial to building trust and understanding with people from different cultures.

Tip 6. Seek out diverse perspectives: Encourage diversity and inclusion in the workplace and actively seek out diverse perspectives.

Tip 7. Apply learning in real-life situations: Apply what you have learned in real-life situations, practise and make adjustments as needed.

Empathy

Cultural Empathy takes Cultural Competence one step further to allow you to understand and share the feelings, thoughts and experiences of people's cultural backgrounds or positions. It involves being able to put yourself in another person's shoes and relate to and connect with them in a meaningful way.

Again, you can start right now with some simple tips:

Tip 1. Show genuine interest: Show a genuine interest in understanding people from different cultures than yours and their experiences. Ask questions and actively seek to understand their perspectives and how they differ from yours.

Tip 2. Learn about their story: Get to truly know the person and understand their history, language and journey. What made them and their community the people they are today? Once you immerse yourself in their position, ask yourself questions. What would you be like if you shared the same history and culture? What would your upbringing look like? Would your religion be different? Would your values be different?

Tip 3. Embrace uncertainty: Recognise that, like Cultural Competence, Cultural Empathy is a process of learning and growth. You may not fully understand or agree with other people's perspectives. The key is to embrace uncertainty and remain open to learning from people with different cultural experiences than your own.

Tip 4. Continuously educate yourself: No culture is fixed. They change as people change. Make sure you're up-to-date with the current issues shaping a culture, not assumptions that are already outdated.

Tip 5. Practise perspective-taking: Make an effort to understand different perspectives and experiences by actively trying to see things from other people's points of view. It's not easy, but it can be encouraged by role-playing, simulations, or other exercises that help people to experience what it is like to be in someone else's shoes.

Tip 6. Be mindful of your own emotions: Be aware of how your own emotions and culture may influence your interactions with people from different cultures than your own. Practise self-regulation in order to approach cross-cultural interactions with a sense of openness and curiosity.

Tip 7. Build relationships with people across an array of cultures: Building relationships with people across an array of cultures can help deepen your understanding of their specific perspectives and experiences and, more broadly, of the perspectives and experiences of other cultures. Make an effort to connect with people and invest time and energy in developing relationships with them.

Tip 8. Be open to learning from your mistakes: Recognise that you may make mistakes; in fact, you will make mistakes. The key is not to avoid mistakes but to remain open to learning from them as an opportunity to deepen your understanding and empathy.

Tip 9. Reflect on your Cultural Empathy: Reflect on your Cultural Empathy through journaling, self-reflection, or seeking feedback from others. This can help you to identify areas for improvement and to track your progress.

Tip 10. Seek out diverse experiences: Seek out diverse experiences that can help to broaden your understanding of different cultures and perspectives. This might be through travel, volunteering, or participating in cultural events or festivals.

The I.C.E model is a process rather than a goal, so you never reach the 'end', but even starting to put it into practice will make it easier to achieve cultural success. It's difficult to base NX campaigns without using I.C.E. as a platform.

Visit lexigo.com/nx for more helpful resources

Build a Case

Don't mistake the Cultural Iceberg, Competency and Empathy ideas we've just explored with some kind of impractical idealism. There's a compelling business case for NX. As the world becomes increasingly interconnected, communicating authentically to audiences in their native language is no longer a 'nice-to-have' business strategy. It's become crucial. The question is no longer whether to engage with audiences in a way that's native to them. The question is 'How'?

You already know that; otherwise you wouldn't be reading this book. However, convincing key decision-makers in your organisation to invest in NX efforts might require a well-structured business case based on the bottom line. This section will guide you through building a compelling argument, highlighting critical factors such as understanding your audience, evaluating current efforts, leveraging data and metrics, and aligning your strategy with C-level objectives.

(Alternatively, you could simply give the decision-makers you need to persuade a copy of this book or direct them to discover more at lexigo.com/nx.)

A series of key steps will give you the necessary insights and tactics to effectively advocate internally for thoughtful NX:

Step 1. Know your audience: The first step in creating a compelling case for NX efforts is to identify your target audiences. Are you aiming to reach local communities in their own language, or are you venturing into a new international market? Understanding your audience is essential to help you tailor your strategy and messaging effectively.

Step 2. Review your in-language efforts: Next, take stock of your organisation's current translation and in-language communication efforts. How well do you reach and engage with different cultural and linguistic communities? Identifying gaps and potential areas for improvement is an effective way to highlight the need for a more focused NX Design Strategy.

Step 3. Highlight key case studies and influencers: Highlight past case studies or key people related to translation and in-language communication efforts. Success stories within the organisation serve as powerful evidence of the potential business benefits of expanded efforts.

Step 4. Review content organisation: Review how content is currently organised across different mediums. Are there platforms or channels where your in-language content could be more effectively displayed or promoted?

Step 5. Identify key decision-makers: Identify the key decision-makers you need to get on board for NX and tailor your business case to address their priorities, anticipating the concerns they may have. Demonstrate how an NX Strategy can help achieve their objectives.

Step 6. Align with C-level goals: You can't build your case unless you understand your organisation's C-level goals and how an NX Strategy can align with and advance them. You need to be able to demonstrate a direct correlation to get buy-in from top management.

Step 7. Assess in-language and translation capability: Evaluate your organisation's readiness in terms of in-language capabilities and translation. Do you have the necessary resources and technology to effectively communicate with different linguistic and cultural communities? If not, include plans for building these capabilities in your business case or how you'll partner with organisations that can provide these capabilities.

Step 8. Use the numbers: Numbers speak volumes. Gather data and prepare metrics that demonstrate the effectiveness of in-language communication efforts, such as increased engagement, higher conversion rates, or improved customer satisfaction scores among in-language audiences.

Step 9. Analyse the competition: Research and compare other organisations in your industry that have successfully deployed similar campaigns. Use these examples to benchmark possibilities and show how your organisation could benefit from a similar strategy.

Step 10. Identify new opportunities: Your proposed campaign could open new doors for your organisation. Identify these potential opportunities and base a business case on how they could contribute to your organisation's growth and success. Identify potential opportunities for cost savings and other advantages that could result from in-language campaigns and show how these financial benefits outweigh the initial investment in NX marketing.

Step 11. Increase capability: Discuss how in-language campaigns can increase organisational capabilities through improvements in technology, talent, or other resources. These changes offer the organisation long-term benefits beyond the immediate marketing campaign.

Me Encanta: An NX Success Story

A well-structured business case for NX Marketing aligns with your organisation's C-level objectives. It highlights the potential for enhanced engagement, increased capabilities, cost savings, revenue, and a stronger competitive position. They are the basis of a compelling argument for the value and importance of NX Marketing.

If you need an example of what success looks like in practice, you don't have to look much further than your local McDonald's.

McDonald's excels in providing an authentic experience to its customers based on a simple secret sauce. They put in the effort to innately understand each of their audiences in order to create experiences that cater to the unique needs and preferences of each customer group—a native experience.

One example came in their home market in the United States, when the business recognised the growing buying power of Hispanic consumers and made a strategic decision to appeal directly to it by developing a distinct marketing approach.

Rather than simply translating their ads to Spanish, they customised their messaging to align with the cultural values of Hispanic consumers, integrating elements such as the significance of family and community into their advertising campaigns.

One of their successful strategies was the 'Me Encanta' ('I'm Lovin' It') campaign, which demonstrated McDonald's commitment to understanding and integrating into Hispanic culture by producing commercials that represented the Hispanic lifestyle, using Spanish-speaking actors and culturally relevant situations.

The marketing approach was wildly successful. Not only did McDonald's see a significant increase in sales among Hispanic consumers, but the company also forged a strong emotional connection with its new demographic.

That was the reward for investing in genuinely understanding their audience and realising that marketing was not simply about translating a message into their language but about authentically reflecting their culture.

For more NX stories like this one, visit lexigo.com/nx or listen to the lexigo.com/podcast

Say Hello to Your NX Teams and Stakeholders

With your well-structured business case approved, congratulations are in order!

You've taken the first major step towards launching an NX strategy. It's time to move on to the next critical phase: assembling the team that will serve as the bedrock of your campaign efforts.

Generally, your NX teams and stakeholders will consist of four primary groups:

NX Teams and Stakeholders	Description
NX Core Team	The primary drivers of your NX initiatives.
NX Advisory Team	An external sounding board that reflects outside perspectives.
NX Ambassador Team	The most authentic layer, the bridge between your campaign and your audiences.
NX Audiences	The communities, organisations and individuals that represent your target audiences.

All teams play critical roles in your strategy, and it's important to understand their composition and responsibilities—and that they might change. It's important to value all team members in an inclusive approach because once NX design starts, it can be a highly fluid process in which the initial team or teams may evolve, and their composition and responsibilities may shift.

Open communication and clarity about roles and expectations at each stage are crucial to ensuring that all team members feel empowered and engaged, regardless of how long they might be involved in the project.

NX Core Team

The NX core team drives your NX initiatives at the highest level, including planning, executing and overseeing the strategy to ensure its success. When assembling this team, consider the following qualities:

Representation: Look for individuals within your organisation who can authentically represent your in-language audiences. This representation helps ensure your campaign resonates with the target audience and accurately reflects their experiences and cultural nuances. This is not always possible, of course, especially in the early stages of your NX journey. In that case, the very minimum you should ensure is that your core team has a high level of Cultural Intelligence.

Diversity and Cultural Competence: Seek out team members who bring diverse and impartial perspectives to your campaign. Cultural Competence—the ability to interact effectively with people of different cultures—is a valuable skill in this context.

Buy-in: Ensure each team member is committed to the campaign's goals. Shared enthusiasm and dedication can significantly contribute to the overall success of your marketing efforts.

Accountability: Empower your team with clearly defined roles and responsibilities, as well as achievable goals. This accountability is key to maintaining a focused and productive team.

NX Advisory Team

The NX Advisory Team serves as an external sounding board for your campaign. They have their finger on the pulse of cultural change, so they can offer outside perspectives, validate your approach and provide the necessary expertise to ensure cultural sensitivity and appropriateness.

When identifying potential advisory team members, consider:

Internal and external stakeholders: Identify internal and external stakeholders who could offer valuable insights to your campaign. This could include organisational leaders, community leaders, local influencers, or industry experts who deeply understand the cultural contexts you aim to engage in.

Peak organisations: Engage with peak organisations or industry bodies within the communities you're marketing to or within the field of products or services you provide. These organisations often have a broad reach and deep understanding of their community, making them valuable partners in your marketing efforts.

Translators: Professional translators will ensure your campaign message is accurately and appropriately conveyed in different languages while also ensuring that cultural nuances are understood and respected. They are the first step in avoiding the marketing blunders we saw from HSBC and Coors.

Language Service Providers (LSPs): LSPs offer services from translation and localisation to interpreting and content creation. Engaging with an LSP such as LEXIGO can help you deliver your campaign message effectively across different languages and cultures.

NX Ambassador Team

The NX Ambassador Team is perhaps the most authentic layer of your NX strategy, serving as the bridge between your campaign and each of the communities you aim to engage. These are individuals who not only understand the culture; they are active, respected members of their communities.

By the way, don't be fooled into thinking that one 'diversity hire' can serve as a catch-all representative for multiple communities. That approach won't work—it also does a disservice to the range of cultures and experiences that make up our global landscape. Each community comes with its own set of values, traditions, and communication nuances that cannot be authentically represented by a single individual tasked with embodying 'diversity'.

This is where the concept of Native really comes into play. It's crucial that each member of your team authentically represents their respective community. This ensures that the insights and perspectives they bring to the table are genuinely reflective of the communities you aim to engage with, allowing for a more nuanced and effective strategy.

Their role is to embody the NX framework at all stages—being Native, Authentic, Trusted, Inclusive, Versatile and Evolving—in real time, on the ground and in the digital sphere.

Key Qualities to Consider for NX Ambassadors:

Native Experience: Choose individuals who are actively engaged in their respective community.

Their credibility lends weight to your campaign, making it more likely to be received positively.

Cultural Fluency: These ambassadors should be fluent in the language, customs and nuances of the community. They are your cultural translators, interpreting and translating language as well as sentiment, behaviour, and expectations.

Passion for the Brand: Ambassadors should have a genuine affinity for your brand or product. This ensures that their advocacy comes across as authentic rather than forced.

Communication Skills: Effective communication is key. Ambassadors should be adept at conveying your brand's message in a way that is both compelling and culturally sensitive.

Adaptability: The landscape of community sentiment and cultural trends is ever-changing. Your ambassadors should be versatile enough to adapt to these shifts and provide real-time feedback to your NX Core and NX Advisory teams.

An NX Success Story

Building strong and diverse NX teams is instrumental to the success of your NX strategy. By ensuring your team represents a variety of perspectives, is committed to the campaign's goals and has clear roles and responsibilities, you'll set a solid foundation for an impactful and resonant NX initiative.

What does a representative, carefully assembled team look like in action? One example comes from London. In 2018, Nike launched its 'Nothing Beats a Londoner' campaign to celebrate and inspire the British capital's young athletes while acknowledging the dynamic and diverse culture that defines the city.

The campaign was driven by a team that reflected London's diverse identity. Nike worked closely with stakeholders ranging from local London-based creatives to athletes, musicians and influencers to authentically capture the spirit and grit of the city's young sportspeople. They also collaborated with Wieden+Kennedy London, an agency with a deep understanding of the local culture, to create a series of short films. Each film featured local athletes, both amateur and professional, overcoming challenges that were specific to the boroughs where they lived.

The campaign resonated strongly with Londoners, earning 3 million views on YouTube in its first week and winning several advertising awards. It remains an excellent example of how an effective and diverse team can create an authentic, impactful campaign.

Sustainability: Building an NX Network

If you want to take your NX design a step further and have ongoing sustainable engagement with different communities, it's possible to develop a Native Experience Network.

In LEXIGO's journey towards fostering sustainable engagement with diverse communities, we created the NX Network, a dynamic database of culturally and linguistically diverse community members and organisations to whom we can turn for advice. We can rely on the Network to give individuals and organisations from target communities a platform for their voices to be heard. The Network helps us understand communities more deeply to shape our communication strategies and enhance community outcomes.

The Network allows us to deliver projects that are tailored and responsive to current trends and apply innovative engagement that goes beyond the one-size-fits-all approach to one that is rooted in the context of each community, resulting in more nuanced and tailored messaging.

A testament to the power of collaborative, culturally informed communication, the NX Network embodies our commitment to speaking to communities, listening to them, understanding them, and amplifying their voices. This is the heart of Native Experience Marketing—a journey towards more empathetic, inclusive and effective communication.

Recap

▶ By investing in your own cultural intelligence, building a strong business case, and assembling a diverse and talented team, you can lay the foundation for creating a truly notable campaign.

▶ The insights gained from understanding the cultural iceberg, the power of diverse perspectives and the importance of cultural empathy will guide your journey towards providing impactful and authentic native experiences.

▶ Armed with these tools and a clear vision, you are ready to embark on a remarkable and memorable journey that resonates with your native audiences.

CHAPTER 3

Be Authentic

'Authenticity is the best marketing strategy there is.'
—GARY VAYNERCHUK, *Serial entrepreneur and businessman*

OK. AFTER CHAPTER 2, you've set yourself up, your NX strategy is approved, and your NX teams are ready to go. Congratulations! It's time to start setting up your campaign for success. And that starts with your audience.

Everyone in marketing was taught to understand the golden rule: 'Know your audience'. But it seems that fewer marketers pay attention to it nowadays. So few brands engage in authentic marketing to thoroughly understand who they are talking to. Brands and organisations think carefully about communications at the language level—the words they use and the ideas they express—but they rarely give deep consideration to what lies beyond that: the people who will hear or read their message.

Important aspects of your audience to consider include the language they speak, their country of origin, their religious affiliation and whether or not they come from a minority background.

Aside from language, communication is about context and culture. It's about finding the best way to understand the audience—its issues, shifts and growth—and to communicate the message to them authentically.

Communication without the right cultural context can cause problems because brands typically apply their viewpoint inappropriately. As an example, most in-language communication is done with an emphasis on the needs of the individual rather than the group. This kind of nuance, however, tends to be distinctly Western. Many (though not all) non-Western societies are founded on collectivist cultures centred around the family unit or community collaboration, where cooperation, dependency and contributing are all more prevalent behavioural expectations.

Brands and organisations that ignore those cultural and contextual distinctions to focus on individual success or satisfaction will not deliver messaging framed correctly for the audience's cultural background.

This chapter helps fill the gap. It will give you the

techniques and models to gain an authentic understanding of your audience that will set you up for the next stage of your Native Experience (NX) journey, using the NX Ambassador team to lean on your highly accurate modelling of the audiences you'll target.

Getting authentic in-language marketing right doesn't just mean avoiding the kind of embarrassing translation errors we saw in the last chapter. The literal translations need to be right—but so does the entire context of the language and its surrounding culture. This is where you need to truly understand your audience's native experience.

NATIVE COMMUNICATION = CONTENT + CULTURE + CONTEXT

FCK It: An Authentic Ad

In 2018, fast-food giant KFC faced a logistical nightmare in the UK when a chicken shortage forced the closure of many of its beloved restaurants. How did KFC respond to the challenge? They decided to embrace it rather than evade it. They temporarily rebranded their iconic logo to 'FCK', openly admitting their 'chicken crisis'. This move was a stroke of marketing genius and a masterclass in authenticity. It demonstrated to KFC customers that they were not afraid to be vulnerable and real. They leveraged humour and humility to turn a potentially disastrous situation into an opportunity to connect with their audience on a deeper level.

It's a story that underscores the power of authenticity in crisis management, showing that, at times, saying 'FCK' can be more effective than pretending to have all the answers. And doing it in a way that resonated with British humour and culture.

Start with Research

Like every other marketing campaign, NX relies on data. Whether it's analysing click-through rates, audience demographics, or customer feedback, data provides the compass by which a campaign charts its course. This data isn't just helpful guidance for NX—it's the difference between success and failure.

There are two broad types of data:

- ***Quantitative*** data offers a bird's-eye view, presenting numbers, percentages and measurable metrics that track behaviours and preferences. It answers the 'how many' and 'how often' questions.
- ***Qualitative*** data dives deeper, exploring the 'why' behind behaviours. It captures sentiments, feelings and motivations.

You need both types of data to paint a complete picture. For instance, while quantitative data might show a high engagement rate among Hispanic audiences during a particular festival, qualitative data might reveal the sentiments, traditions and values associated with that festival, guiding marketers on how best to approach this segment.

Utilising data grants you a window into your

audience's world, revealing what they hear, see and experience daily—our main objective in this phase.

It sheds light on the conversations they're immersed in, the visuals they're surrounded by, and the experiences shaping their perspectives. That way, data moves beyond statistics to unfold the very fabric of their environment, enabling marketers' messages to resonate on a more authentic and personal level.

Understanding and connecting with your NX audiences means stepping into their shoes, grasping their worldview and appreciating their values. Data acts as the bridge to this understanding. With precise data:

- You can tailor campaigns to resonate deeply, ensuring cultural symbols are used correctly and respectfully.
- You can identify potential pitfalls or areas of cultural sensitivity, avoiding missteps that could alienate audiences or even cause offence.
- Most importantly, you can discern genuine insights into the values, aspirations and needs of different cultural groups, allowing for the creation of campaigns that truly reach, include, engage and convert audiences to grow your initiatives.

In a moment, we'll explore what type of data will help us get the most authentic perspective and how best to collect it. Before we do that, however, we need to revisit our NX Ambassador team. They're the representatives of each individual community, audience or language group, and they'll be instrumental in helping us sift through our data to ensure we're concentrating on the right information.

It's a common misstep for organisations and brands to lump 'ethnic', 'foreign' or 'multicultural' audiences together in a single monolithic entity. Such an approach is overly simplistic and fundamentally flawed. Each community or language group is a distinct audience with its own cultural norms, values and communication styles. To treat them as a single, homogenous group is to miss the forest for the trees.

The only thing these diverse groups share is the virtual 'bucket' into which they're all placed. To truly engage with these audiences, it's imperative to approach each as its own unique entity, deserving of a tailored strategy and individualised attention.

That's why the NX Ambassador team is so important at this stage. They can help gather data and ensure that it's the right data, which distinguishes between each audience. Indeed, throughout the whole NX experience, the NX Ambassador team will help prevent a campaign from slipping into the trap of lumping 'ethnic', 'foreign' and 'multicultural' audiences together because they're at the heart of their communities.

The ambassadors' responsibilities, now and throughout the whole process, include:

- **Community Engagement:** Ambassadors are responsible for engaging with the community both online and offline, ranging from social media interactions to attending community events.
- **Feedback Loop:** They should provide regular feedback to the NX Core Team, offering insights that only a native community member can provide. This feedback is invaluable for course-correcting the campaign strategy as needed.
- **Content Validation:** Before any campaign material is finalised, ambassadors should review it to ensure it aligns with community values and expectations.
- **Crisis Management:** In the event of a cultural misstep, ambassadors are your first line of defence, helping to manage community reactions and offering immediate solutions.
- **Local Partnerships:** Ambassadors can identify potential local partnerships that could amplify your campaign, such as collaborating with community organisations or local influencers.

Gathering Insights with Quantitative Data

There is a wide range of effective methods to gather quantitative data. Depending on your objectives, budgets and time, you may want to consider the following:

Surveys and Questionnaires: Structured questions to gather numerical data on preferences and behaviours.

Publicly Available Data: Utilising government statistics, market research reports and academic studies for demographic and market-size information.

Social Media Analytics: Using built-in analytics tools on platforms such as Facebook and Twitter to gather data on user behaviour and demographics.

Web Analytics: Tools like Google Analytics to track user behaviour, engagement and conversion rates on websites.

Consumer Purchase Data: Analysing sales records to understand buying patterns within different cultural groups.

Cultural Dimensions

A particular concept worth mentioning with respect to quantitative data is *Hofstede's Cultural Dimensions Theory.* Developed by Dutch psychologist Geert Hofstede, this framework uses six dimensions to understand the differences in culture across countries and communities, including your NX audiences. Identifying the varying degrees of importance of each dimension helps marketers speak the language of their audience and create messaging that resonates deeply with ingrained cultural norms—enhancing the effectiveness, reach and engagement of your NX campaign:

> **PDI/Power Distance:** Here we measure the degree to which inequality in power distribution is accepted by the less powerful in a society. A high PDI indicates a societal acceptance of a hierarchical order and significant disparities in power and wealth, often akin to a caste system where social mobility is limited. Conversely, a low PDI suggests a society that values equality and challenges the disparities in power and wealth, promoting a more egalitarian structure where hierarchy is downplayed and power is distributed more democratically.

> **IDV/Individualism:** IDV assesses the relationship between the individual and the larger social

groups. In societies with high IDV scores, there is an emphasis on personal achievements, autonomy and individual rights, with social relationships being a matter of personal choice and often subject to change. In contrast, societies with low IDV scores hold community and familial interdependence in high regard, where individuals are expected to act in the interest of the group and maintain strong, long-lasting bonds within their communities.

MAS/Masculinity: This dimension highlights how much society does or does not strengthen the traditionally held notion that men are the main achievers and power brokers in society. A high score would suggest that the society is less focused on ensuring gender equality and more on traditional gender success factors, such as achievement and competition predominantly associated with male roles.

UAI/Uncertainty Avoidance: The Uncertainty Avoidance Index (UAI) gauges a society's comfort with uncertainty and the unknown. A high score on this dimension indicates a low tolerance for ambiguity, leading to a preference for well-established structures and clear rules. In such societies, there is an emphasis on formal procedures and a need for consistency and detailed planning to mitigate the anxiety of uncertainty.

LTO/Long-term Orientation: This dimension reflects a society's perspective towards time and the extent to which actions are influenced by this perspective. A high score in LTO indicates a culture that is oriented towards the future and values perseverance and prioritises long-term success over immediate gratification. Businesses in such societies may be more welcomed if they show a commitment to long-term development and sustainability. They must balance this, however, with respect for the enduring traditional values that may coexist with progressive attitudes towards change and innovation.

IND/Indulgence vs Restraint: This dimension explores the extent to which a society allows for the free gratification of natural human drives related to enjoying life and having fun. A high score in indulgence indicates a society that allows relatively free gratification of desires and fosters an atmosphere of optimism. On the other hand, a low score in this dimension signifies a culture that suppresses gratification of needs and regulates it through strict social norms.

Hofstede's cultural dimensions offer a strategic lens through which you can fine-tune your efforts to suit different cultural landscapes. For instance, in a society with a low individualism score, you might shift your messaging focus from individual benefits to communal or family advantages. This could manifest in various ways, from packaging that emphasises shared experiences to advertising narratives that highlight community or family values.

> ***Author's note:*** *When your NX audiences are local or in-country communities, the key when analysing cultures against the varying dimensions is to understand the balance the community has between their heritage culture and their home culture. For example, newly arrived migrant communities are likely to possess more of their heritage culture than well-established migrant communities.*

Discovery Through Qualitative-Data Methods

Understanding the Cultural Iceberg

Gathering initial qualitative data on the communities you intend to reach relies on the diverse perspectives, unique expertise and insights of your NX teams.

We've seen in the previous chapter that gathering insights is like exploring an iceberg. To coin a phrase, we'll dive deeper into the concept here. At first glance, you may only see the tip of the iceberg: the surface characteristics of a culture, which are important but only reveal a portion of the whole.

To connect deeply and authentically with your audiences, you need to go beneath the surface, exploring unseen cultural elements such as values, beliefs, traditions and communication styles. This deep understanding forms the foundation of effective NX implementation.

Surface Characteristics: The Visible Part of the Iceberg

The surface characteristics of a culture are those immediately identifiable traits that often spring to mind when we think of a particular community. These can include:

- language
- food

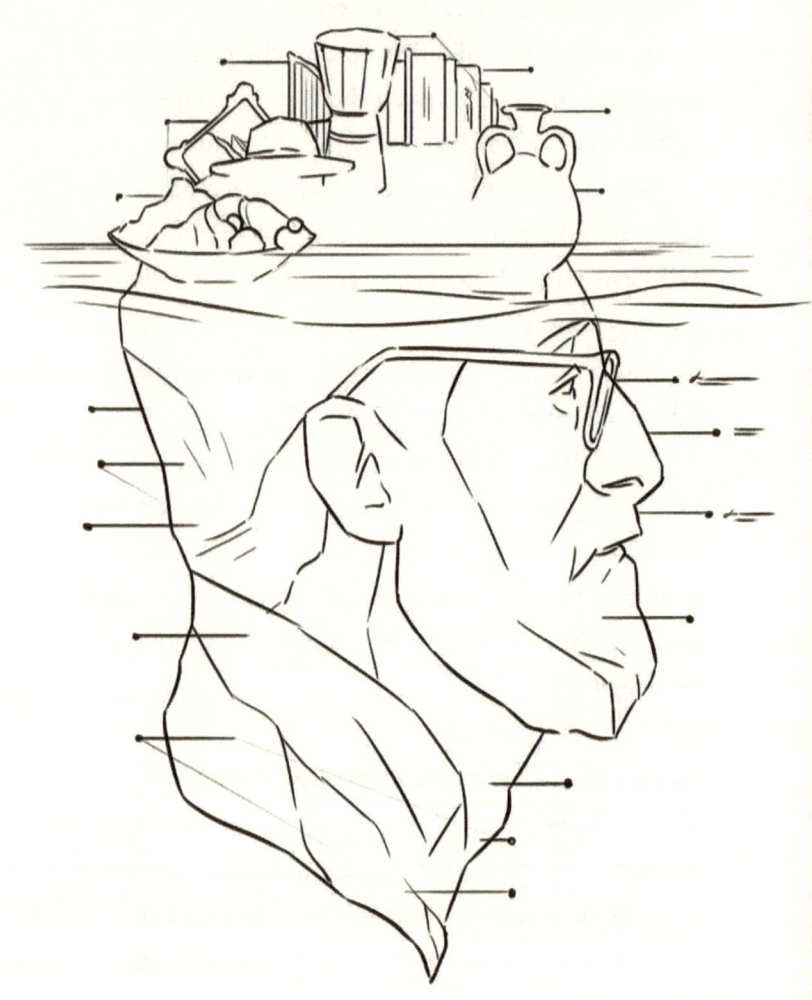

- dress
- customs
- music
- flags
- festivals.

These traits, while important, only provide a snapshot of a culture. They are the tip of the cultural iceberg.

Deep Culture: The Hidden Part of the Iceberg

Beneath the surface lies the larger, unseen portion of the iceberg, representing the deeper aspects of culture:

- beliefs
- values
- communication styles
- religion
- concepts (e.g. of time, of family, of work)
- traditions
- and much more.

Being sensitive and respectful towards these deep cultural elements is vital to avoid messages being ignored or perceived as insensitive.

Diving Deeper

With this understanding of the cultural iceberg, it's time to begin gathering insights. We'll start by exploring various cultural groups and communities, defining the key characteristics of each to ensure our marketing efforts connect effectively.

Utilising available qualitative data, we will:

Analyse Cultural Nuances: Research and understand the preferences and communication styles of our target audiences. We'll also delve into any existing data to gain a better understanding of our audience.

Assess Communication Channels: Review the effectiveness of existing communication channels and identify gaps and opportunities for improvement. This assessment includes understanding culturally relevant channels specific to each community.

Understand Stakeholders: Understand the roles and positions of key stakeholders involved in the process, such as campaign working groups, community organisations and peak bodies.

These insights will help shape our messaging and

choice of communication channels and provide the basis for further research. They're the foundation of our NX strategy.

By taking the time to educate ourselves and adapt our approach to each group, we'll remove language barriers and create a stronger connection between these communities and our brand.

Remember, effective NX is about more than translation; it's about understanding the whole cultural iceberg.

Listening to Native Experiences: The Human Element in NX Research

In NX, listening to people with native experiences is a powerful tool to add depth and nuance to your research. While quantitative data provides the broad strokes, listening to people who are true members of your audiences in the research stage allows you to zoom in, capturing the subtleties and complexities that numbers alone can't reveal.

People's voices offer a qualitative counterpart to the quantitative data you've gathered.

NATIVE EXPERIENCES ARE NUANCED AND NUANCE CREATES AUTHENTICITY

NX Voice Forums: The New Age Focus Groups

I remember the traditional focus groups we used to conduct in my early years at LEXIGO. They were effective but often felt like a one-sided interrogation. The participants would share their thoughts, sure, but the environment was more clinical than conversational. It was as if we were extracting information rather than engaging in a dialogue.

Fast forward to today, and we've transitioned to what we call *NX Voice Forums*—these sessions a fundamental shift away from the old focus-group model. We no longer get participants to answer the questions we want to ask. We listen to what they want to say so we can ensure their voices are heard.

Why Use NX Voice Forums?

Apart from providing a wealth of qualitative data, capturing sentiments, beliefs and attitudes that can inform your NX strategies, NX Voice Forums are a more effective approach than a traditional focus group for the following reasons:

Factor	Traditional Focus Group	NX Voice Forums
Purpose	Gather targeted feedback on specific questions.	Encourage open-ended dialogue and listen to unprompted feedback.

Factor	Traditional Focus Group	NX Voice Forums
Environment	Often structured and formal, with a one-way flow of information.	Informal and conversational, fostering a two-way exchange.
Participant Role	Respondents answer predefined questions.	Active contributors sharing spontaneous insights.
Moderator Role	Directs the discussion with specific questions.	Facilitates the discussion, allowing natural flow.
Outcome	Data-driven insights based on direct questioning.	Holistic understanding through authentic conversations.
Emphasis	On obtaining answers.	On understanding native experiences, lived experiences and perspectives.
Engagement	Passive participation with guided responses.	Active engagement with encouragement to initiate topics.
Data Collection	Quantitative leaning, with qualitative elements.	Primarily qualitative with an emphasis on narrative.
Feedback Nature	Can be limited by the questions asked.	More diverse and potentially more insightful.
Session Flow	Linear, following the moderator's guide.	Organic, led by the participants' interests and priorities.
Cultural Sensitivity	May not fully capture the subtleties and nuances of a culture.	Designed to uncover and respect cultural nuances, providing a more accurate reflection of diverse audiences.
Actionable Insights	Insights may be constrained by the narrow focus of the questions.	A relaxed environment nurtures honesty, yielding deeper and broader insights that inform actionable strategies.

Author's note: *I don't say much about the concept of 'lived experience' in this book, but I do want to draw attention to its potential relevance in your NX campaigns. Lived experience typically refers to the knowledge and insights individuals gain through their direct, day-to-day experiences, particularly those shaped by unique and often profound circumstances. The term is often associated with discussions around disabilities, trauma, social justice issues and other significant life challenges.*

I want to acknowledge the weight this term may carry especially in fields such as healthcare, social work and psychology, where it is used to understand and empathise with the experiences of individuals facing significant life challenges. If you're engaged in sectors where personal trials and triumphs are paramount, taking account of lived experience can be crucial in understanding and connecting with your NX audience. It's especially pertinent when conducting the NX Voice Forums I'll discuss later, or developing campaigns for culturally and linguistically diverse audiences.

If your work intersects with areas where lived experiences are particularly telling, they can deeply enrich your approach to engaging with specific communities and guide your strategies to be more empathetic, relevant, and impactful.

Structuring an NX Voice Forum

Structuring your own NX Voice Forum is straightforward—and well worth the effort. Here are some brief tips to get you started, but for a detailed plan, visit lexigo.com/nx:

Diverse Representation: Ensure that your sessions are representative of the cultural demographics you aim to target. This might mean having separate forums for different cultural communities.

Cultural Moderators: Work with moderators who are skilled in facilitating discussions and are culturally aware of the community they are working with. Ideally, moderators should even be members of that community.

Language Accessibility: Make sure that language barriers are minimised. This could mean offering translation services or conducting the whole forum in the native language of the participants.

NX Voices and the Cultural Iceberg

NX Voice Forums help you explore beneath the surface of the cultural iceberg model. They can reveal the values, traditions and social norms that drive audience behaviour.

For instance, if your *quantitative* data shows that a particular cultural group has a high preference for organic products, a well-structured NX Voice Forum can help you understand why. Is it a deep-seated cultural value, a trend, or perhaps a reaction to a specific event or issue?

The best way to reveal such insights is to plan and use your NX Voice Forums as part of a series of steps:

Plan: Outline the objectives and questions you aim to explore.

Recruit: Use your quantitative data to identify the right participants.

Execute: Conduct the NX Voice Forum, ensuring cultural sensitivity and inclusivity.

Analyse: Collate the findings, looking for patterns or insights that can inform your NX strategies.

Integrate: Combine these qualitative insights with your quantitative data to create a more comprehensive and authentic NX strategy.

NX Voice Forums are more than a research tool. They're a bridge to understanding the cultural landscape of each community you're navigating. They offer a human element, giving faces and voices to the numbers and percentages. Most importantly, they provide the 'why' to your 'what', enabling you to create NX campaigns that truly resonate.

Other Methods of Gaining Qualitative Data
Of course, Voice Forums are not the only way to gather qualitative data. Many other means can be effective, including some that are established tools in the marketer's armoury.

> **In-depth One-to-one Sessions:** In-depth, one-to-one interviews serve as a cornerstone in the qualitative research toolkit, offering a focused and intimate setting to explore the complexities of individual perspectives. Unlike NX Voice Forums, where group dynamics can sometimes overshadow individual voices, one-to-one sessions provide a confidential space for participants to share nuanced opinions, beliefs, and experiences.
>
> This method is particularly valuable in NX research into sensitive or taboo topics, as it allows for a deep dive into the cultural subtleties that shape audience behaviour. Skilled facilitators can adapt their questions in real time, steering the conversation into areas that may not have been initially

considered but emerge as significant. For example, an in-depth interview with a member of a specific cultural community could reveal unique insights into the role of family, tradition, or even spirituality in purchasing decisions. These rich, textured insights complement quantitative data, adding an understanding that numbers alone cannot provide.

Ethnographic Studies: Ethnographic studies—the study of people in their own environment—immerse researchers directly into the daily lives and cultural contexts of diverse communities. They provide a lens to view what people say, what they do and why they do it. Researchers observe and sometimes participate in the routines, rituals and interactions that define a community, capturing implicit behaviours and unspoken norms that might not surface even in interviews or focus groups.

For example, an ethnographic study of shopping behaviours among a cultural group might reveal the importance of community recommendations or the role of traditional beliefs in product selection. These insights are invaluable in crafting campaigns that resonate on a deeply authentic level. The holistic view we get from ethnographic studies can help to fill any gaps left by quantitative data and add a rich layer of context.

Case Studies: Detailed investigations of specific instances or scenarios, often involving multiple data sources such as interviews, observations and documents based on past efforts or other sources that might be helpful for your current efforts.

Open-ended Surveys: Surveys with open-ended questions allow respondents to answer in their own words, providing more nuanced insights.

Sentiment Analysis: Analysing text from social media, reviews, or other platforms to gauge public opinion and emotional tone on specific subjects.

In this chapter, we've seen how research, particularly when filtered through an NX Ambassador team, can help marketers achieve authenticity in each of their markets. It's important to remember, however, that authenticity is not a destination. It's not something we achieve once and forget; it's something we have to achieve constantly as a vital part of a larger process. It prepares the ground for meaningful NX relationships. For those relationships to grow into loyal customers and advocates takes more than just authenticity; it takes trust, and that's where we'll turn our focus next.

Recap

- Communication goes beyond language and involves taking into account the context and culture in which it occurs. It's only by understanding context and culture that you can achieve the kind of authenticity that will make your message resonate with your intended audience.
- Your authentic perspective relies on research, which can include all sorts of culture analysisand can be more or less useful depending on the specific situation.
- Quantitative data can reveal a lot about the motivations and preferences of different cultures, but qualitative research is more effective in revealing those parts of the cultural iceberg that lie beneath the surface, such as beliefs, values and traditions.
- NX Voice Forums are different from traditional focus groups. Rather than getting participants to answer the questions you want to ask, you offer them a platform for what they want to say, creating a more dynamic and, ultimately, more valuable source of qualitative data.

PHASE II:
DESIGN

NOW THAT WE'VE PUT together our building blocks and laid out the fundamentals needed for a successful NX campaign, we're ready to start *relationships* and *researching* and *preparing* and *creating* our campaign through a structured creation process.

Trust lays the strategic groundwork, while inclusivity brings that strategy to life through creative execution. This section is best implemented in an iterative cycle so you only move once you have completed the cycle: TRUSTED then INCLUSIVE, then back to TRUSTED, then INCLUSIVE until you're happy with the result.

In CHAPTER 4: BE TRUSTED, we'll start to create a successful NX campaign that draws on all the groundwork we laid in the THINK stage. By using our new knowledge, working with our team and armed with the tools and tactics needed to co-create a successful NX campaign, we'll look at how to set our objectives with regard to the audience landscape. We'll also consider what personas and channels to use to develop our strategy.

CHAPTER 5: BE INCLUSIVE helps prepare your campaign for launch. You'll use all the information you gathered in CHAPTER 4 to create an inclusive strategy that allows you to develop deeply inclusive creative elements using a process of structured co-creation with your audience.

CHAPTER 4

Be Trusted

'Do the right thing as marketers to build trust.'
—JON DICK, *VP Marketing, HubSpot*

IN 2007, I FOUND myself in Collins Street, Melbourne, killing time before a pivotal meeting. Born and bred in a city renowned for its coffee culture, I was a 24-year-old coffee snob. I had even dabbled as an amateur barista in my younger years. So, when I saw a newly opened Starbucks up the road, I was sceptical. But with only $3 to lose and time to kill, I decided to give it a go. The experience was both enlightening and amusing.

'Can I please have a small latte?' I enquired, wallet in hand.

'We don't have small,' replied the partner, which is what Starbucks calls their baristas.

I was intrigued. 'OK, what sizes do you have?'

'Tall, grande and venti,' the partner answered, gesturing to the cup sizes on display.

'Do you have anything smaller than this?' I asked, pointing to the Tall cup.

'Yes, we have a Short,' the partner said, reaching for a smaller cup hidden beneath the counter.

'Great, then I'll have a latte in your smallest cup size, please.'

Just Because it's Venti, it Doesn't Mean it's Trusted

The interaction was a fascinating study in cultural disconnect. The partner was clearly following a script that had been imported wholesale from the United States. The problem? The script didn't resonate with me—and therefore, probably not with the whole Australian audience. By importing an American playbook into an Australian context, Starbucks had failed to achieve authenticity, one of the key pillars in the NX framework.

The result? You guessed it: a rapid erosion of trust, culminating in the closure of 250 Australian Starbucks stores in 2008.

Several years later, the story took another turn. An Australian organisation acquired the Starbucks franchise in Australia. It reopened the stores, adopting a hyper-localised strategy that was authentic to the Australian market and the Starbucks brand. It reestablished trust, and today, you'll find around 70 Starbucks across the country.

The Value of Trust

Welcome to the foundation of any lasting relationship: trust. In a world where consumers are bombarded with choices, trust is the compass that guides them to your brand. It's what transforms a one-time buyer into a lifetime customer, a passive observer into an active advocate. It is also the starting point for building an NX Strategy that resonates deeply with audiences through careful use of trust signals.

Trust signals are literally signs that indicate to the consumer that a brand has the credibility to be trusted.

They can include everything from the messaging to the design of your packaging. Failing to consider these elements in your initial strategy can lead to costly mistakes, as one food giant discovered when it tried to break into the African market.

The large multinational launched its line of baby food in Africa with packaging that featured a picture of a cherubic baby. In Western countries, this image is seen as endearing, evoking feelings of innocence and purity. However, in many African cultures, the norm is for the packaging to display the contents of the can. Of course, no one believed the can contained food that was actually made out of babies, but the image led to confusion and outright aversion among local consumers. The trust signal they thought they were sending was, in fact, a signal of disconnect.

The fallout was immediate. Sales plummeted, and the multinational had to backpedal to correct a mistake that could have been avoided with a more 'trusted' approach to market entry. This example serves as a cautionary tale for any brand looking to expand its global footprint. Trust is not one-size-fits-all; it must be carefully cultivated to fit the cultural and social norms of each specific market.

Trust Signal	Description
Fonts	Fonts should be easy to read and culturally appropriate, as some scripts or styles may carry different connotations in different cultures. For example, it's pretty easy to spot 'Made in China' products by simply looking at the packaging and their use of a Times New Roman style font.
Colours	Brands should choose colours that align with cultural meanings and aesthetic preferences to build trust with their target audience.
Images	It's essential for brands to ensure that their visual content reflects the values and diversity of the community they engage with.
Humour	It is important for brands to use idioms, sayings, and cultural expressions carefully to avoid any offence.
Channels	Brands should opt for popular and trusted channels within their target communities, such as social media, traditional media, or local events.
Accessibility	Making content accessible for people with disabilities is a trust signal demonstrating a brand's commitment to inclusivity. This includes subtitles, alt text for images, and assistive technology compatibility. By paying attention to these aspects, aligning them with the community's preferences and being culturally sensitive, brands can establish strong trust signals with their audience.
Quality Certifications and Awards	Certifications and awards are trust signals that indicate a brand has met certain standards and been acknowledged by third parties for quality products or services.
Digital	Digital trust signals such as social media accounts, online support, a well-designed website and professional packaging can signal that a brand is legitimate and cares about its image and customer experience.

Next time you're looking at an ad or content or picking up a product and feel like it doesn't connect with you, take some time to examine it and see which trust signals are missing. Even the smallest detail can make a significant difference—you'll be surprised at how much.

Navigating Cultural Landscapes in Strategy

Starbucks missed the mark by the slightest detail; the food giant by overlooking a larger consideration. Both stories remind us that crafting a strategy isn't just an act of ticking boxes or simply moving a model from one country to another that speaks the same language. Language similarities can be deceptive: the same words can have different implications in different places, thanks to deep cultural nuances, significantly impacting consumer trust.

Gaining trust is a strategic endeavour requiring meticulous planning, research and understanding. The value of a robust strategy in this area can't be overstated. With a clear strategy, organisations can navigate the complexities of different cultural landscapes, avoid harmful stereotypes and genuinely connect with their audiences on a meaningful level. The strategy provides

TRUST SIGNALS ARE CULTURALLY CODED

a roadmap, ensuring that every initiative aligns with the overarching objectives, remains culturally sensitive and achieves the desired impact.

Crafting an NX Strategy

Establishing a strategy begins by understanding the primary objectives you want to achieve and assessing the intricacies of the audience landscape. Without this foundational understanding, marketing efforts risk being disjointed or, even worse, culturally insensitive.

Let's look more closely at the two critical stages of crafting an NX strategy.

#1 Overarching Objectives

Before continuing our Native Experience (NX) journey, we need to identify our destination. What is the ultimate goal? What does success look like? What are we aiming to achieve? How do these objectives relate to the Notable goals we set for the campaign? We lay out our objectives using SMART goal setting:

> **Specific:** Clearly outline what the campaign aims to achieve. This might include metrics such as engagement rates, conversions, or increased brand recognition within certain cultural communities.

Measurable: Set quantifiable targets. Instead of just aiming for 'increased engagement', specify a percentage increase or a specific number to reach.

Achievable: Ensure the goals are realistic, given the available resources and timeframe.

Relevant: Ensure the objectives align with the broader goals of the organisation, catering specifically to NX audiences.

Time-bound: Define the timeline. When should specific milestones be reached, and by what deadline should the overall objective be accomplished?

Understanding these objectives provides a roadmap for PHASES 2 and 3 of your NX journey and establishes the criteria by which its success will be measured.

#2 Assessing the Audience Landscape

Once your objectives are set, it's crucial to understand the 'terrain' the campaign will be executed on: the audience landscape. This involves:

Demographic Understanding: Begin by understanding the size, distribution and growth rates of different cultural groups in the target market.

Which communities are dominant? Which are emergent? What are the age distributions within these communities? Such insights help tailor campaigns to the most relevant audiences.

Cultural Nuances: Each culture has its own set of values, beliefs, traditions and taboos. By understanding these, you can craft messages that resonate deeply and avoid causing offence. For instance, colours, symbols, or even certain numbers can have varied connotations across cultures.

Community Dynamics: Beyond broad cultural understanding, it's essential to recognise community-specific dynamics. How do different cultural communities interact with each other? What are their primary sources of information and influencers within their communities? What platforms or channels are they most active on?

Crafting a Culturally Informed NX Strategy: From Objectives to Personas and Messaging

By combining the clear direction provided by well-defined objectives with insights gained from assessing the audience landscape, we're now in a position to develop a comprehensive NX strategy tailored to the campaign goals and target audiences.

We'll do this by building *personas*, identifying the appropriate *channels* and tactics for reaching each cultural group and creating an *engagement* framework that incorporates cultural nuances and ensures relevance and resonance across targeted audiences, communities and language groups.

As we'll see in the next chapter, these same three building blocks will be used to drive our co-creation efforts when we start working directly with our audiences.

> ***Author's note:*** *Audience definitions, while essential, can't be rigid constructs. Like NX itself, they are dynamic and adaptable. As we transition into the next stage of our framework, Inclusive, our initial definitions may evolve as we introduce LEXIGO's co-creation approach. There, we won't just be identifying our audience, we'll also be learning from them and adjusting our approach based on their feedback and insights.*

Personas

Armed with the insights and discoveries gleaned from the Authenticity phase, we're well-positioned to construct personas based on authentic evidence of our NX audiences. Just think of the people who were involved in your NX Voice Forums; some were a fit and others, frankly, were not. Creating accurate and insightful personas helps us understand and leverage the unique qualities of different cultures so that we can tailor messaging and strategies to resonate with target audiences.

Developing personas will help us identify the right people to include in co-creation at the *Inclusive* stage, as described in the next chapter.

Numerous persona frameworks are available, but the key is to create personas that are both authentic and culturally nuanced. They should not be demographic sketches. They should encapsulate the unique identities and complexities of different cultures. In terms of our NX strategy, we should consider several factors:

> **Conduct Thorough Research:** To create effective personas, you need thorough research to understand your target audience's cultural nuances and values. Research should go beyond surface-level demographics to examine the nuances of cultural identity, language, and religion—the submerged part of the cultural iceberg (all the details described in CHAPTER 3: BE AUTHENTIC).

Find Commonalities and Differences: Use your research to identify commonalities and differences between your target cultural groups. This will help you create personas that accurately represent your audience's values, beliefs and interests.

Test, Update and Refine Your Personas: Test your personas using real-life examples and lean on the NX team you've been developing for further insight and feedback. You can only stay current with cultural shifts and changes if you continuously update and refine personas.

Step Into Their Shoes: Consider what personas might say and what actions they might take. What are their thoughts and feelings as they navigate their day? What challenges do they face in their environment? By spending a figurative day in their shoes, you gain invaluable insights that help you craft a persona that is emotionally and psychologically attuned to the nuances of the audience you aim to engage.

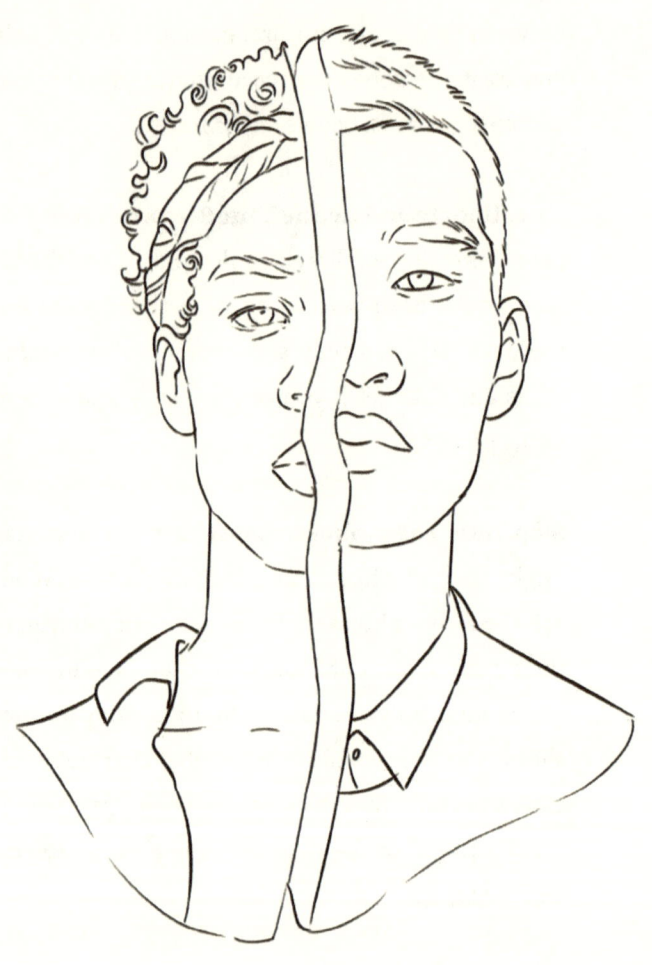

To ensure the creation of authentic and effective personas that will help lead to a trusted strategy, we check our personas against *LEXIGO's 3Rs Persona Criteria*:

Relevant: This criterion includes basic demographic information such as gender, age and generational cohort. These factors help segment the audience but are just the starting point.

Representative: Beyond demographics, we include elements such as family structure, type of employment and native language. These elements should be representative of the broader demographic and cultural context.

Resonant: This criterion focuses on emotion and psychology. Does the persona resonate with the audience? Can they relate to this individual? Is the persona a true representation of their community or cultural background? Emotional and psychological authenticity will lay the groundwork for a strategy that communicates effectively and fosters genuine engagement.

> ***Author's note:*** *There's an inherent danger with using personas that they become a type of stereotype or generalisation of cultural groups, which is the complete antithesis of what we're trying to achieve. To create relevant and authentic marketing strategies, acknowledge the unique identities of different cultural groups by using personas purely as a tool. Given the fluid nature of culture and cultural identities, it's vital to continuously revisit, update and refine your personas to make sure they remain current.*

Channels

Placing your campaign on channels used by your chosen target audience will increase your reach and ROI. Many people worldwide use WhatsApp to communicate with loved ones overseas, for example. If you're targeting audiences from mainland China, consider Chinese social media channels. This is also a good time to think outside the box of traditional media outlets.

Speaking through channels they trust and resonate with, rather than using generic marketing strategies that may miss the mark, is necessary to reach the heart of a community by:

Researching: Understand where specific cultural groups predominantly consume information. Is it a community radio station? A regional newspaper? Or even a local influencer on social media?

Tailoring: Use your research to customise the mode and medium of communication. For instance, younger members of a community might be more receptive to digital campaigns, while older demographics might respond better to traditional media, which we'll cover soon.

Ultimately, our choice of channel is a strategic extension of the personas we've developed. It's about meeting our audience where they are, both literally and metaphorically, and communicating in a manner that is both culturally sensitive and resonant.

Some of the channels and approaches that you may want to consider across Traditional and Digital Channels include:

Traditional Channels

When considering the efficacy of various media channels in reaching NX audiences, specialist in-language newspapers and community-specific traditional media outlets stand out for their ability to deliver higher ROI.

These platforms cater to a niche but highly engaged audience, offering a direct line to communities often overlooked by mainstream media. The readers of these publications are typically deeply connected to their cultural roots and communities and value content that resonates with their specific experiences and perspectives. As a result, advertising or featured content in these outlets is likely to be more relevant, more engaging and more effective.

In May 2022, Australian free-to-air television station SBS launched a new multilingual news channel, SBS WorldWatch. The launch reflected the fact that 5 million Australians—almost 20 per cent of the population—speak a language other than English. For brands and organisations looking to improve their communication with culturally and linguistically diverse audiences, the appeal of buying against such programming is clear.

Along with multilingual TV stations like SBS WorldWatch, Australia also has 17 paid and streaming television stations in seven languages for Chinese, Vietnamese, Filipino, Indian, Arabic, Italian and Greek communities, more than 100 radio stations broadcasting in-language radio programs, and around 200 print publications covering 47 communities.

That kind of market share makes it worthwhile for brands and organisations to put more effort into marketing to audiences in their own language. Communicating with these audiences is about more than ticking the 'translation' box, however. Communication with non-English speakers isn't just an afterthought. It requires just as much effort, if not more, than communication written in English.

The targeted nature of more specialised media channels means that your message reaches those who are most likely to respond, providing more efficient use of marketing budgets and a greater potential for meaningful engagement and conversion.

Type	Approach
Community Engagement	Engage with local communities. Trust is built through direct, face-to-face interactions in many communities. Brands can foster this trust by collaborating with local cultural groups and community leaders who already have established relationships within their communities. A grassroots approach builds trust and provides invaluable cultural insights.
People of Influence	Partnering with people of influence who genuinely represent your target communities can extend your reach and lend trust to your brand. It's about discovering voices that resonate with the unique identities within these communities, beyond just focusing on numbers.
Cultural Festivals, Events and Sponsorships	Participation in cultural festivals, events and sponsorships that promote your target community's work and efforts can significantly expand a brand's reach. It's an opportunity to align your brand with values that resonate with your target audience and show support to the communities.
Podcasts	Collaborating with podcasters who focus on community-specific topics or concerns can offer a more intimate way to engage with your audience. Podcasts provide a platform for deeper discussions and storytelling, adding another layer to your marketing strategy.

Native Experience Marketing

Type	Approach
Community Radio Stations	These stations are often the heartbeat of local communities, broadcasting in various languages and catering to diverse cultural groups. They are ideal for reaching specific audiences with tailored messages that resonate with their cultural background and daily lives.
In-Language Newspapers and Magazines	These publications serve as trusted sources of information for non-English speaking communities. They offer a platform for culturally relevant content and advertising, allowing brands to connect with audiences in a language they are most comfortable with.
In-Language Television Channels and Services	These channels provide entertainment and news in specific languages, making them a powerful medium to reach NX audiences. Advertisements and sponsored content on these platforms can effectively engage viewers in their native language.
Public Relations and Community Outreach	A dedicated effort in public relations, focusing on building relationships with community leaders and participating in community events, can be very effective. This includes giving interviews to local media, participating in local talk shows, or writing articles for local publications.
Local Community Partnerships	Forming partnerships with local community organisations or leaders can be an effective channel. These partnerships can facilitate better understanding and direct communication with the target cultural groups.

Digital Channels

Type	Approach
Social Media Platforms	Be social on social media. Platforms such as Instagram, Twitter and Facebook offer opportunities for diverse representation and direct engagement with various community groups. They serve as a modern agora, a public space where dialogue and exchange happen in real time.
Email Marketing	Personalised, in-language emails can be a powerful tool for engaging specific segments of your audience. Tailoring your message to align with different demographics and cultural identities adds a layer of personalisation that generic campaigns often lack.
Content Marketing	Creating content such as blog posts, videos and infographics that address a range of topics relevant to your target communities can further enrich your brand's narrative as long as it is both informative and culturally sensitive.
Podcasts	Collaborating with podcasters who focus on community-specific topics or concerns can offer a more intimate way to engage with your audience. Podcasts provide a platform for deeper discussions and storytelling, adding another layer to your marketing strategy.
Educational Programs and Workshops	Offering educational content or workshops that are relevant to specific cultural communities can be an effective way to engage. These can be conducted both digitally (through webinars, online courses) and traditionally (in community centres, schools, or through local organisations).
Mobile Marketing	Mobile marketing through apps, SMS, or messaging platforms in native languages can be a direct and personal way to reach NX audiences. This approach allows for targeted messaging and offers based on cultural preferences and behaviours.

A key piece of advice when targeting NX audiences and markets is to avoid relying solely on one type of media channel.

The true potential lies in the harmonious integration of both traditional and digital channels. Consider using digital channels to amplify your traditional efforts or, conversely, complement your digital strategies with traditional media. This integrated approach can create a more comprehensive and impactful reach.

Keep in mind that the channels listed here are just a starting point; the possibilities are vast and varied. Experimenting with different combinations and strategies can unlock unique advantages and opportunities for reaching and resonating with NX audiences.

Case Study: Cultivating Trust and ROI through Cultural Targeting: ANZ's Introduction of Asian Banking Managers

In 2009, ANZ, one of Australia's largest four banks, made a decision to deepen its connection with one of the fastest-growing demographics in the country: Chinese-Australians. This strategic move was both a step towards inclusivity and a smart business decision rooted in understanding the power of cultural resonance and trust in banking services.

Recognising the increasing significance of the Chinese migrant population in Australia, ANZ identified a unique opportunity to meet this community's needs better. Its primary goal was to provide Chinese customers with a seamless and culturally sensitive banking experience, enhancing customer satisfaction and building long-term loyalty, thereby increasing the return on investment (ROI) through community-focused services.

With Mainland China emerging as a significant source of immigration, ANZ recognized that many Chinese Australians continued to maintain business operations in China while managing their financial needs in Australia.

It introduced specialist Asian Banking Managers in 16 branches across key Australian cities. These managers were fluent in Mandarin and Cantonese, and served as primary contacts for Chinese Australians within ANZ's branch network, bridging language and cultural gaps. This initiative was supported by ANZ representatives in Beijing, Shanghai, and Guangzhou, who allowed customers to establish banking relationships with ANZ even before moving to Australia. The bank complemented this initiative by introducing accessible phone banking services and an online resource for locating branches where Chinese languages were spoken, ensuring that language was never a barrier in the banking experience of Chinese Australians.

The introduction of Asian Banking Managers led to several positive outcomes:

- ***Enhanced Customer Experience:*** *Customers experienced banking in their native language, leading to a more comfortable and trusting relationship.*
- ***Community-based Marketing****: Word-of-mouth marketing within the tight-knit Chinese community amplified the effectiveness of this initiative.*
- ***Increased ROI:*** *By targeting a specific community with tailored services, ANZ tapped into a niche market, leading to higher customer retention and attracting new customers through trusted community networks.*

ANZ's strategy is a compelling example of how targeting specific communities with culturally and linguistically tailored services can increase trust, customer satisfaction, and, ultimately, higher ROI.

Messaging

There are many potential frameworks we can use for our messaging, depending on our goals. Many of them sound like anagrams from crossword clues. Some of them include—take a deep breath—AIDA, PAS, BAB, PPPP, CCCC, FAB, QUEST, CIRCLES, STAR, OATH, SOAP and AICPBSAWN. There are many, many more.

The fact is that what model we use is less important than how it fits into the overall NX framework. At

LEXIGO, our work means we often favour the AIDA (Attention-Interest-Desire-Action) model to drive us to a culturally informed audience journey.

In this stage, we are yet to really develop any final messaging. Instead, we'll be working with our NX Ambassador team to come up with key messaging and engagement ideas to bring to the table with our audiences in the *Inclusive* stage of NX, where we will further develop our personas, channels and messaging through a co-creation approach.

AIDA model

Using the AIDA model, our NX Ambassadors will draft messaging around:

Stage	Audience Mindset	Objective
Attention	This speaks to me.	Gaining attention isn't just about flashy ads or catchy slogans. It's about cultural resonance. The first touchpoint must resonate with the specific cultural nuances, languages, and values of the target audience. This could mean using imagery that reflects the community, language that speaks to them, or channels that they frequent. The goal is to make them stop and think, 'This speaks to me'.

Stage	Audience Mindset	Objective
Interest	This is something I want to learn more about.	Once you have your audience's attention, the next step is to pique their interest. This is where the insights from the Authenticity stage and your personas come into play. Tailor your messaging to address the unique needs, questions, or problems that your target cultural group might have. The aim is to move them from 'This speaks to me' to 'This is something I want to learn more about'.
Desire	I need this.	Creating desire in a cultural context requires a deep understanding of what different communities value. Is it family? Tradition? Innovation? Social status? Use these audience insights to frame your product or service as something that can fulfil these specific desires. Your goal now is to make them think, 'I need this'.
Action	What's the next step?	The final step is to prompt action. This could mean different things for different cultural groups. For some, it might be a direct call to action ('Buy now'), while for others, a softer approach like 'Learn More' or an invitation to a community event might be more effective. Whatever that next step might be, whether it's making a purchase, signing up for a newsletter, or attending an event, the key is to make it easy for them to take.

We need to ensure that our message reaches our target audiences while effectively resonating with them. Some best practices can help with drafting your messaging:

Understand Cultural Priorities: What motivates a particular cultural group? Is it community welfare, individual achievement, or familial bonds? If you understand these intrinsic motivators, you can craft messages that align with them.

Avoid Stereotyping: Don't use clichés or generic cultural references. Personalise and customise content to reflect genuine understanding and respect.

Localised Content: Reflect the local realities and sensibilities of each audience or community, which might involve incorporating local dialects, idioms, or even culturally significant visuals.

Collaborate with Community Leaders: Engaging local leaders or influencers can provide credibility and extend the reach of campaigns within specific communities. It's a good idea to bring them in early.

Avoid One-size-fits-all: Recognise and respect the diversity within communities and language groups. Even within a broader cultural group, nuances can differ significantly between individual communities.

Reaching out isn't the same as just broadcasting a message; it establishes a genuine connection. With the right personas, channels and messaging, you can make a lasting positive impression, setting the stage for deeper engagement and considerations when you scope your strategy.

Scoping out your strategy

As we finalise the strategic groundwork in our NX journey, bear in mind that we haven't created a final blueprint but a flexible framework to guide us in the next stage, *Inclusive*. Establishing trust with our audiences is a delicate process, so while we're still making initial contacts and gathering real-time insights, we need to keep our strategy adaptable.

Making sure we select the right channels, craft action-centric content and maintain cultural relevance through our personas, the co-creation we'll do in the next stage will bring us faster to our ultimate goal: inspiring desired behaviours and fostering deeper connections with diverse communities.

Think of your strategy as a hypothesis—an informed hypothesis shaped by extensive research and insights—rather than something set in stone.

Scoping out a strategy involves laying down a preliminary plan based on the data, insights and personas that have given you a thorough understanding of the cultural, social, and personal values of your audience, forming the foundation of trust. This understanding shows the kind of commitment to meeting their specific needs and preferences that is indispensable for earning trust.

Your focus should be on defining the current market position and the unique value proposition of your brand. Understand where your brand sits within the cultural landscape and how it can relate to the audiences you want to engage with. To truly connect with your intended audiences, you start by exploring the environment where you are.

It's less about who your audience is demographically and more about who they are culturally, linguistically, socially and behaviorally. Understanding the environment gives you a compass to track the ebb and flow of market dynamics in terms of both observable surface behaviours and deeper undercurrents.

Above all, remember that our strategy *is* a compass, not our map. It guides us but remains open to any new paths that emerge as we move into the Inclusive stage of our NX journey.

When you scan the environment to take the pulse of your NX audience, bear these considerations in mind:

Cultural Sensitivities and Nuances
- awareness of cultural holidays and events
- historical context affecting perceptions
- language preferences and nuances.

Market Sentiment and Trends
- prevailing opinions about your industry
- influential social or political events
- trends in consumer behaviour within different cultures.

Community and Social Factors
- community leaders and influencers' stance on your brand
- social issues resonating with the audience
- economic conditions affecting the audience.

Legal and Regulatory Environment
- regulations affecting communication or product offerings
- compliance requirements for different markets
- data protection and privacy concerns.

How, then, can you accurately assess your current brand position? Tools like SWOT (Strengths, Weaknesses, Opportunities and Threats) analysis offer a panoramic view of your strengths and reveal the chinks in your armour—the weaknesses where waves could break through. Market segmentation and consumer insight studies refine your understanding of the cultural isles you wish to explore. Real-time feedback and sentiment analysis, gleaned from listening tools and social-media analytics, grant you a glimpse into the ongoing dialogues and the emotional pulse within these communities.

Other factors to look at include:

Company Culture and Values
- alignment with diversity and inclusion
- employee diversity representation
- internal communication effectiveness.

Brand Health and Equity
- current brand perception within diverse markets
- past marketing campaigns' success and failures
- brand consistency across markets.

Operational Readiness
- adaptability to market changes
- infrastructure for multilingual support
- resource allocation for market research.

Change Management
- anticipated restructures or policy changes
- ongoing training programs for inclusivity
- leadership's openness to new strategies.

An introspective look at your brand's reputation and the trust you've built up across different cultural groups is also important here. Trust is a currency that varies in value across the societal spectrum and is shaped by historical experiences and social narratives. By gauging trust levels, you begin to unearth the barriers to and the catalysts for engagement within each community.

Setting the Stage for Inclusion

As we wrap up this chapter, let's take a moment to acknowledge the ground we've covered. We've delved deep into the elements of trust: transparency, credibility, consistency, emotional connection and cultural nuances. We've developed personas and channel strategies and explored the AIDA framework to draft messaging tailored to our audiences and objectives.

Let's be honest, however: as comprehensive as they are, these efforts only provide us with a blueprint—our NX Design. It remains a theoretical framework that is yet to be tested and validated. The real work, the true test of our strategy's efficacy, lies ahead in the next chapter.

It's where we engage in co-creation, working hand-in-hand with the very communities we aim to serve. We've taken a lot of care to craft our personas, channel strategies, and trust elements. Now is the time to put them to the test as we build and create content not just for but in collaboration with our target communities.

As we prepare to turn the page, it's worth remembering a truism: a strategy untested is a strategy unproven. The next two chapters aren't just another phase but *the* phase. It's the crucible where our plans will be refined, validated and, ultimately, brought to life.

So get ready to roll up your sleeves and get stuck in. The most exciting part of our journey—for me, anyway—is about to begin.

Recap

- Trust is how you ensure that your message doesn't just communicate with your audience but resonates deeply with them.
- An informed NX strategy is built on a foundation of the objectives you want to achieve and the terrain in which you're operating.
- Construct personas to ensure that you've accurately identified your target consumers and ensure that you've selected the best channels to communicate with them effectively.
- Use messaging frameworks such as AIDA (Attention, Interest, Desire, Attention) to ensure that your messaging is both consistent and on-target.
- Your NX strategy is a blueprint that only exists on paper; now it's time to try it in the real world.
- In any relationship, first impressions set the tone for future interactions. In NX Design, this is especially significant. The first message a cultural group receives from an organisation can either foster trust or sow seeds of disconnect.
- This is especially important for your initial outreach to work with your audiences in the design phase. Ensuring that the initial contact is

respectful, informed and relevant is paramount. We need to make sure we're armed with a baseline strategy to take with us and truly make our strategy trusted and inclusive.

- This is when we scope out our strategy to identify the goals for the campaign to take us into the rest of our NX journey. Armed with your data, insights and personas, you can start with comprehensive research to understand the cultural, social and personal values of your audience. This forms the bedrock of trust as it shows commitment to meeting their specific needs and preferences.
- Focus on defining the current market position and the unique value proposition of your brand. Understand where your brand sits in the cultural landscape and how it relates to the audiences you intend to engage with.

CHAPTER 5

Be Inclusive

*'Diversity is being invited to the party;
inclusion is being asked to dance.'*
—VERNA MYERS, *Vice President of Inclusion Strategy, Netflix*

WELCOME TO THE CRUCIBLE!

This is where the meticulous planning, strategising and blueprinting we've covered in the last three chapters are put to the test. This is where we transition from the drawing board to the real world, from theory to practice.

If trust is the strategic cornerstone of our Native Experience (NX) campaign, as we've just seen, then inclusivity is its creative lifeblood. Inclusivity is not an afterthought in co-creation; it's the very essence. It means we will speak with them, not about or at them. In this way, you can work together to develop creative elements that are visually and emotionally compelling—of course, because that's what you do!—but also deeply resonant with the communities you aim to engage.

We'll explore how to bring the elements of trust into our creative process, ensuring a cohesive and impactful campaign. More importantly, we'll look closely at the transformative power of co-creation. Our carefully crafted personas, channel strategies and trust elements will be put to the ultimate test as we build and create content not just for but in collaboration with our target communities.

In 2023, Cricket Australia had a goal of making cricket a sport that unites and inspires all Australians, irrespective of their cultural background, and launched a carefully planned campaign to achieve that aim.

The campaign began with a multi-faceted research process designed to understand the different communities Cricket Australia wanted to reach, particularly South Asian communities whose cultures have a strong cricket tradition. It encompassed various methods, such as desk-based research that combined analysis of internal records and external data sources. Further broadening the scope of insights, a comprehensive survey was sent to community respondents. This survey reached an impressive 27,000 responses from individuals, a testament to the widespread engagement and interest in shaping the future of cricket in Australia.

This deep dive into data laid the groundwork for a more nuanced understanding of the participation patterns and experiences of various communities in cricket.

To add a layer of authentic experiences, the data collection was rounded off with engaging and insightful focus groups, offering an intimate space for deeper discussion and exploration of the specific experiences and needs of individuals in various facets of cricket, offering a window into the attitudes of cricket players, fans, and volunteers in Australia.

Each data collection method was as important as the next to understand cultural differences and behaviours in cricket and inform an inclusive Multicultural Action Plan that succeeded from the very outset of engaging the target communities.

The Pillars of Inclusive Creative

It's crucial to have a set of guiding principles that inform our co-creation with our target communities. These principles serve as the bedrock upon which we build creative elements that are compelling and truly inclusive. They ensure that diversity is actively embedded in every facet of our campaign, rather than just paying lip service to the idea.

In this section, we'll discuss the four pillars that form the foundation of truly inclusive creative. None of the pillars stand alone; they combine to form a holistic approach to inclusivity.

Cultural Representation: In a diverse world, representation goes beyond featuring diverse faces in your advertisements and calling it a day. It extends to storytelling, the nuances of social interactions, and the contexts in which your products or services are used. If you don't represent this diversity, you miss an opportunity and potentially alienate potential customers who don't see themselves in your brand narrative. From imagery to idioms, ensure that content mirrors the aesthetics and lexicon with which the target audience is familiar.

Language and Communication: Language is more than a tool for communication; it is a reflection of culture, identity and community. Ensuring that your messaging is linguistically accessible is just the starting point. The challenge lies in making it culturally resonant. This involves going beyond language to understand idioms, humour and references that are meaningful to each cultural group you're targeting. Your message can't only be translated. It needs to be 'transcreated'—adapted to its specific audience while maintaining its intent, tone and context.

Accessibility: Inclusivity is functional as well as cultural, which means that campaigns must be accessible to people with different abilities, be they visual, auditory, or cognitive. This might mean considering text readability, offering alternative text for images, or providing captions for videos, among other things. It can be tempting to see accessibility as a 'nice-to-have'. Not so. In today's world, it's a 'must-have'. Today, no one can afford to exclude a segment of their audience with consequences.

Community Engagement: The final pillar of inclusive creative is perhaps the most dynamic: community engagement. It's about augmenting market research or social listening with active collaboration with community members through NX Voice Forums, social media polls, or community events. This type of active engagement allows you to co-create creative assets that are well-received from the start.

These four pillars serve as the guiding principles for developing creative elements that are visually and emotionally compelling; and deeply resonant with the diverse communities you aim to engage. But they're just the first step. The real magic happens when we bring these principles to life through co-creation.

Bridging the Pillars and the Process: Why Co-creation is Non-negotiable

Bringing the pillars of inclusive creative to life requires one of the most profoundly impactful concepts in the NX Experience: co-creation. Co-creation is the vehicle that takes us from concept to reality. It's the alchemy that transforms our well-intentioned strategies into authentic, resonant creative elements.

What is co-creation? Simply put, it's creating your NX campaign alongside the audience it's for. Why is it non-negotiable in truly inclusive marketing? It ensures that our creative elements are theoretically sound and practically effective because they have been vetted by the very communities they aim to serve.

Co-creation is our 'how'. It's the mechanism that breathes life into the 'what' of guiding pillars, transforming them from abstract ideals into tangible realities.

Co-creation is transformative for three reasons:

- It brings the title of this entire chapter, *Inclusive,*

to the forefront. When you co-create with your target communities, you're creating what will resonate, instead of just guessing. This eliminates the risk of cultural missteps and ensures that your campaign is rooted in genuine understanding.

- Co-creation fosters a sense of ownership among community members. When people see that their voices are heard and actively incorporated, it engenders a level of trust and loyalty that is hard to achieve through traditional top-down approaches.
- Co-creation is a powerful tool for innovation. The collective intelligence of a community often uncovers insights and ideas that would be difficult to achieve in isolation. It's a symbiotic relationship where both the brand and the community stand to gain.

By embracing the power of co-creation, you're adding another tool to your marketing toolkit and adopting a new way of thinking that recognises the exponential value of community intelligence and diversity in authentic representation.

How to Co-Create

Co-creation requires a tailored and flexible approach that considers the unique characteristics and needs of each community. However, we at LEXIGO have developed a method based on five universal stages that can help guide any co-creation journey:

1. Groundwork
2. Co-creation sessions
3. Messaging
4. Creative
5. Test and refine

Stage 1. Groundwork

Identify Community Stakeholders

Before you can co-create, you need to know who to co-create with. By this stage, you know the languages and communities you're working with, so now we need to start by identifying community leaders, influencers and everyday grassroots members who can provide valuable insights.

> **Mapping Stakeholder Networks:** Use tools such as stakeholder maps to visualise the network of people and organisations that will be involved. This can

help in understanding the dynamics and relationships that might influence the co-creation process.

Cultural Sensitivity: Given that you're dealing with diverse communities, it's crucial to be culturally sensitive in your approach. Research the community's history, values and norms to better understand how to engage them effectively.

Voices Heard/Challenge Personas: We can refer back to the Authenticity stage to ensure that the people involved in our listening sessions match our defined personas and that we have a good sample of participants who are a true representation of their community.

Your NX Ambassadors should already have all this knowledge or know where to find it. They are an integral part of the co-creation process. In fact, they should own the majority of it.

NX Ambassadors
Gather your NX Ambassador team and assign facilitators. They should know how to facilitate inclusive sessions or assist a community facilitator in guiding the sessions.

Inclusive Session Training: While your facilitators are community insiders, it's essential to train them in the art of leading inclusive sessions. They already have cultural competency, of course, but they still need to master techniques to ensure that all voices are heard and that the co-creation process is equitable. Training could cover aspects such as active listening, conflict resolution and how to encourage quieter members to share their perspectives.

Technology and Tools: Decide on the technology and tools that will be used during the co-creation sessions. Make sure they are accessible to all members of the community, keeping in mind varying levels of technological literacy.

Set Clear Objectives

Knowing what you aim to achieve is the compass that guides your co-creation journey. Whether you're developing a new product, refining an advertising campaign, or creating community programs, having clear objectives will keep you on track.

- Lean on the strategy you developed in the last chapter to ensure your objectives are aligned and SMART (Specific, Measurable, Achievable, Relevant and Time-bound).

- Ensure that the objectives of the co-creation process are in sync with the broader business goals of your organisation or project—this will help move your co-creation efforts from a standalone initiative to an integrated part of the larger strategy.

Stage 2. Sessions

With your community collaborators identified and your objectives established, the stage is set for the real magic to happen. Whether you're hosting brainstorming sessions, workshops, or virtual meet-ups, the goal of your co-creation sessions is to develop concepts that are innovative and deeply resonant with your target communities. These sessions should be safe spaces where ideas can be freely shared and critiqued.

Create a Collaborative Environment

Creating the right environment is crucial for success. While digital platforms like specialised forums or social media groups offer convenience and scalability, I always advocate for physical spaces such as community workshops when possible.

Physical spaces often foster a level of engagement and spontaneity that virtual environments struggle to replicate. They allow for 'watercooler moments'—those unplanned, serendipitous interactions where some of the best ideas often emerge. The key is to make it easy for community members to contribute, providing a safe and relatable space for honest conversations and workshops.

By emphasising the value of physical spaces, you're offering a venue for collaboration; you're creating an ecosystem where creativity and community can flourish in their most authentic forms.

> **Accessibility:** Ensure that the chosen platform or venue is accessible to all community members. This includes considerations for physical disabilities, as well as technological barriers for digital platforms.

> **Ground Rules:** Establish a set of ground rules that promote respectful dialogue and equitable participation. Make these rules visible and ensure they are agreed upon at the start of each session.

Acknowledge and Reward

Recognising the contributions of community members is courteous and, more importantly, essential for building long-term relationships and trust. This could be through public acknowledgment, incentives, or even revenue-sharing models for substantial contributions.

> **Transparency:** Be transparent about how

contributions will be acknowledged and rewarded. This sets clear expectations and fosters a sense of fairness.

Cultural Sensitivity: Tailor your acknowledgment and rewards to be culturally appropriate. What is considered a meaningful acknowledgment can vary from one community to another.

Conduct Inclusive Audits

Before embarking on new creative endeavours, take stock of where you currently stand. Evaluate your existing creative assets through the lens of both inclusivity and trust. Are your current assets culturally sensitive? Do they uphold the elements of trust we discussed earlier? An audit will highlight any gaps whilst also providing a baseline against which you can measure future progress.

Audit Criteria: Develop a set of criteria that reflect the principles of inclusivity and trust. This could include language appropriateness, representation of diverse groups and alignment with community values.

Benchmarking: Use the audit to establish a baseline. This will highlight gaps and provide a point of reference against which you can measure future progress.

Stage 3. Messaging

Pre-Session Briefing
Before you start a co-creation session, provide a brief overview of what the messaging aims to achieve. This sets the stage and ensures that everyone is aligned on the objectives.

> **Contextualise:** Explain how the messaging fits into the broader campaign or project.
>
> **Share Objectives:** Reiterate the SMART objectives you set earlier to guide messaging development.

Ideation Phase
This is the heart of the co-creation session for messaging. Encourage community members to share their ideas freely, fostering a brainstorming environment.

> **Prompting Questions:** Use prompting questions to guide the discussion and spark ideas, such as 'What words resonate most with our community?' or 'What message would make you proud to be part of this community?'

Idea Clustering: As ideas are generated, cluster them into themes or concepts that could form the basis of the messaging.

Drafting and Refining

Once you have a set of themes or concepts, start drafting potential messages. Depending on the different campaign elements, these could take the form of taglines, slogans, or key messages.

Collaborative Writing: Use collaborative tools such as shared documents where everyone can see the drafts and contribute in real time.

Iterative Feedback: Allow for rounds of feedback and refinement within the session itself, aiming to narrow your creative down to a few strong messages and ideas by the end.

By structuring your co-creation sessions to include these steps, you can ensure that the messaging developed is creative and deeply resonant with the community. It becomes a collaborative effort that leverages the collective wisdom and insights of the community, making the end result—your campaign messaging—truly inclusive and impactful.

While co-creation is a unique process, it doesn't

operate in a vacuum. It's essential to align your co-created messaging with established marketing frameworks such as AIDA to ensure a cohesive and effective communication strategy.

Stage 4. Creative

As we navigate the co-creative process, it's essential to remember that inclusivity isn't just a strategic consideration—it's a creative one as well. These are the sensory elements that will bring your campaign to life, and they need to be sensitive and inclusive. The elements of trust we meticulously developed in the previous chapter must be seamlessly integrated into our creative process if we're not to risk destroying the trust we have established.

It's as easy as A, B, C:

A. *Cultural Briefing*

Start by providing a briefing that outlines the sensitivities, taboos and preferences related to visuals and aesthetics within the community and validate these with the group.

> **Cultural Dos and Don'ts:** Share insights on colours, symbols and patterns that are culturally significant, as well as those that should be avoided. Test these with the group.

Community Examples: Showcase examples of visuals that have successfully resonated with their community in the past, explaining why they worked.

This step should be natural and integrated if your NX Ambassadors are already familiar with these preferences and elements. Here, we're just validating and testing our ideas to make sure we have our creative asset starting points on the right track so we can refine them to reflect the current environment and sentiment.

B. Visual Ideation

This is the brainstorming phase for visual elements that will appear with the message, where community members can further suggest ideas for colours, patterns, images and other visual aspects.

Mood Boards: Create collaborative mood boards where community members can pin images, colours, or patterns that they feel represent the community well.

Alignment with Messaging: Ensure that the visual ideas generated are in sync with the messaging framework developed earlier, perhaps even revisiting the AIDA framework to see how visuals can enhance each stage.

C. Drafting and Prototyping

Once you have a pool of ideas, start creating draft versions of the visual elements.

> **Collaborative Tools:** Use design software that allows for real-time collaboration and feedback, enabling community members to see how their ideas are taking shape.

> **Iterative Design:** Similar to messaging, allow for rounds of feedback and refinement, ensuring the visuals are culturally sensitive and aligned with the community's preferences.

The 5 Cs

At LEXIGO, we developed a model we call the 5Cs to ensure that creative content is co-created towards inclusivity rather than being dictated or guided down a path that has been pre-determined before the session even takes place.

The 5Cs will give you a comprehensive, easy-to-remember checklist that guides you through the complex but rewarding process of inclusive creative co-creation. Using these five guiding principles is visually appealing, deeply resonant and ethical.

Clarity

Clarity refers to the transparency in your creative process. Be open about the rationale behind your design choices, the sources of your materials, and the lessons learned from any missteps. Transparency fosters trust and resonates with audiences. We hear a lot about transparency these days. More than a buzzword, it's a commitment to openness that can significantly enhance the trustworthiness of your campaign.

This means being open about your creative process, the choices you make and even the mistakes you learn from. Whether it's sharing the rationale behind a particular design choice or disclosing the source of your materials, transparency fosters a sense of integrity that resonates with audiences. Don't be afraid to go back to the drawing board during your session; the creative you may have developed for the session is only a springboard, after all.

Credibility

Your creative elements are an extension of your brand and as such, they need the same level of credibility. This involves ensuring that all claims made in your campaign are verifiable and that your portrayal of different cultures and communities is accurate and respectful. Authenticity is key here; it's what turns a sceptical audience into believers.

Cohesion

Consistency is the glue that holds your campaign together. It ensures that the trust you've built in the strategic phase is not squandered when you transition to creative development. Every visual element, every piece of copy, and every interaction must align with the trust-based strategy developed in the previous chapter. Inconsistencies can erode trust, while a cohesive, consistent message can amplify it.

Connection

Connection goes beyond words and cultures. It's the universal language that turns a campaign from a simple transaction into a meaningful interaction. Weaving emotional intelligence into your creative elements means understanding the emotional nuances of different cultural groups, the triggers that evoke specific emotions, and the stories that resonate on a deeper level. It's less about what you say and more about how you make people feel.

Conscience

Conscience should guide your creative process, stretching all the way from the representation

CLARITY
CREDIBILITY
COHESION
CONNECTION
CONSCIENCE

of different groups to the sourcing of materials and even the platforms where your campaign is displayed. Upholding ethical standards is the right thing to do, and is also good for business.

How do you apply this to your sessions? Here's a practical example that can also act as a checklist for using the LEXIGO 5C framework in your sessions:

LEXIGO 5C Framework	Stage 4. Creative		
	A. Briefing	B. Visual Ideation	C. Drafting and Prototyping
Clarity	Clearly define campaign goals, rationale and desired outcomes.	Maintain open lines of communication for continuous feedback.	Collaboratively assess and refine creative elements based on feedback.
Credibility	Conduct comprehensive research with input from stakeholders to ensure accuracy.	Fact-check visual concepts and ensure they align with the researched information.	Document sources and contributions meticulously for transparency.
Cohesion	Develop a cohesive and unified strategy that incorporates diverse cultural insights.	Integrate diverse insights into visual concepts, ensuring consistency with the overall strategy.	Review and adjust campaign elements to maintain consistency and alignment.

LEXIGO 5C Framework	Stage 4. Creative		
	A. Briefing	B. Visual Ideation	C. Drafting and Prototyping
Connection	Engage in meaningful dialogues to understand the cultural contexts through open discussions.	Identify key touchpoints in the campaign for emotional connections with the audience.	Encourage the sharing of personal stories and cultural insights to deepen connections.
Conscience	Establish clear ethical guidelines that align with the project's values and objectives.	Regularly assess the ethical implications of visual elements and materials used.	Implement mechanisms for ethical oversight and accountability throughout the creative process.

Co-creation thrives in an environment where all participants are seen as equal contributors, regardless of their role or background. This doesn't mean that everyone's ideas are adopted as is, but rather that each idea is given consideration and the space to influence the outcome. When you're transparent about the rationale for decisions (Clarity) and committed to representing cultures accurately and with respect (Credibility), you're on the right path.

To ensure that co-creation in creative is at the heart of LEXIGO's 5C Framework, it may be helpful to ask whether these principles genuinely welcome and integrate the insights and experiences of all co-creators. Are the cultural insights and contributions from various groups heard and allowed to steer the campaign direction? This can often be the difference between a campaign that is created in a spirit of true partnership and one that superficially checks the boxes of inclusivity.

Stage 5. Test and Refine

Once you've completed stages 1–4, it's time to create a set of concepts and assets as you would for any campaign but then instead of going straight to launch, it's time to present your creative back to the community, through NX Voice Forums, online surveys, or community forums. Listen carefully to the feedback and be prepared to have to go back to the drawing board.

This can be tremendously frustrating—trust me, I've been there—but co-creation can be slow because it thrives on iteration. Remember that each cycle of feedback brings you closer to a final product that truly resonates.

Co-creation is not a one-and-done affair but an ongoing process. Establish clear feedback channels for your community collaborators to tell you what they think, and use the insights you gain to continuously refine your creative elements. Don't be afraid to release multiple versions of a creative element based on the feedback received. This iterative approach allows you to fine-tune the messaging until it resonates deeply with the community.

Community Validation
Before finalising the creative elements use a variety of ways to validate them within the cultural context of your target community.

> **Community Review:** Share the drafts with a broader segment of the community, gathering feedback on cultural appropriateness and resonance.
>
> **A/B Testing:** If feasible, conduct A/B tests with different visual elements to gauge their effectiveness in real-world scenarios.
>
> **Mini Surveys:** Use quick polls or surveys to gauge reactions to the drafted messages.
>
> **NX Voice Forums:** If time and resources allow, conduct NX Voice Forums to delve deeper into the community's response.

Finalise Creative Assets
After multiple rounds of testing and refinement, you'll arrive at creative assets that are both inclusive and trust-enhancing—but the work doesn't end there. Once

the community approves the assets, they need to be professionally finalised for the campaign. This could involve high-quality production, localisation for different markets, or accessibility adaptations.

> **Iterate and Refine:** Co-creation is an ongoing process. Use the feedback and insights gained to continuously refine your creative elements.

> **Measure Impact:** Finally, assess the effectiveness of your co-created elements against the original objectives you set. This will demonstrate the ROI of co-creation and provide learnings for future initiatives.

Prepare to GO

By the time your creative assets are ready to launch, you'll be ready, too. The iterative nature of co-creation requires patience and faith, so it's a relief to get to this stage. However, the benefit is that you can be highly confident in your creative and in the initial reception it will receive because you've taken the time to work with your partners in the community. In the next chapter, we'll see how best to manage a launch—and we'll learn that in NX, the launch is not so much a destination as the start of a new journey.

Let's use a case study to illustrate what I mean.

This one is close to home, as it comes from our work at LEXIGO. In 2023, LEXIGO studied 14 separate communities to understand community insights concerning vaccination during the COVID-19 pandemic.

We spoke to more than 150 individuals across the communities, with anonymous online contributions from some 300 people. Community members were empowered to craft messages that genuinely reflected their perspective on COVID-19 and broader health topics, a bespoke approach that marked a significant departure from previous government one-size-fits-all approaches.

This co-creation led to the creation of 1,200 assets—posters, social media messages and tiles, and videos—across five pillars in 14 communities. Implementation was by 95 key individuals, including translators, medical professionals, and people of influence, who could create print materials directing readers to in-language media content. It was all grassroots dissemination, with no above-the-line advertising. We used a range of online platforms as well as direct community engagement.

Recap

- Inclusivity is the lifeblood of campaigns. It has four pillars: Cultural Representation, Language and Communication, Accessibility and Community Engagement. They rely on true co-creation, which gives your community audience a sense of true inclusion.
- Co-creation has five main elements: Groundwork, Co-creation sessions, Messaging, Creative, Test and Refine.
- Co-creation is not quick, it relies on iteration, with constant analysis and refinement. Although this can be frustrating, it produces far more satisfactory results than traditional methods of creating a campaign and imposing it on a community rather than letting the community join the creation process.

PHASE III:
GO

PHASE III: GO IS where we move from strategy to launch—and then continually monitor the effectiveness of our campaign so that we can adapt as necessary.

At this stage, the key is remembering that what can seem like the culmination of the campaign—going to market—is in fact just its beginning. Gathering feedback is essential, and ignoring it would be a mistake. This feedback is the basis for evolving the campaign over its life, following an approach founded on versatility.

In CHAPTER 6: BE VERSATILE, we consider focusing on the dual aspects of launching and measuring a campaign. Companies need to be agile, ready to deploy across various channels and prepared to measure outcomes in real time. Key decisions are selecting the right mix of media, how to allocate resources efficiently and how to set up key performance indicators (KPIs) for immediate measurement.

CHAPTER 7: BE EVOLVING is a natural next step,

emphasising the importance of tracking and measuring the campaign post-launch. Here, the focus shifts from immediate metrics to long-term impact and measuring. This is where companies need to be vigilant about external and environmental factors that could affect the campaign's success.

CHAPTER 6

Be Versatile

'My strength is in my ability to be versatile.'
—WENDY STARLAND, Singer, Songwriter and Producer

IT WAS A 19TH-CENTURY German general who came up with the well-known observation that in military planning, no plan survives the first contact with the enemy. It's the same in any marketing campaign, and Native Experience (NX) is no different. That's why you have to remain alert and versatile when you go to market.

After so much effort has been put into drafting your strategy, co-creating and going back to meticulously shoring up your strategy, it can be tempting to think that reaching implementation—the GO phase—means you've achieved your goal. It's tempting to feel as if the heavy lifting is done and that you simply need to press the go button to execute.

As any seasoned marketer will tell you, going to market is not the end but a new beginning. It takes you into a dynamic, ever-changing landscape that requires versatility and the willingness to be nimble.

In this chapter, we'll explore the art of being Versatile, learning how to pivot when circumstances demand it, and how to optimise opportunities that might present themselves. When used well, versatility is key to effective communication in dynamic markets where communities grow, sentiments shift, and cultural nuances are as fluid as they are intricate.

Cultural norms evolve, market trends shift, news stories break and community sentiments can change almost overnight. In such an environment, a rigid, one-size-fits-all approach is a recipe for failure. As we enter the GO phase, grassroots organisations and community stakeholders become invaluable allies. They offer real-time insights into evolving cultural norms and sentiments that allow us to fine-tune our strategies and messaging.

Being versatile is crucial in responding to changes as they occur. It allows us to fine-tune our strategies, tweak our messaging, and even pivot our entire approach. However, versatility isn't just about reacting to change; it's also about anticipating shifts before they happen, comprehending the underlying factors that influence community attitudes, and having contingency plans in place that can be deployed at a moment's notice. This proactive stance is made possible through continuous engagement with grassroots contacts and stakeholders who serve as our eyes and ears on the ground.

By now, these stakeholders should be prioritised relationships and natural integrations of our NX efforts; if anything, these relationships accelerate here. They offer real-time insights into evolving cultural norms and sentiments that allow us to fine-tune our strategies and messaging.

By keeping these key players and other NX teams as true owners of the process, we enhance the versatility of our campaigns, ensuring that they are, at minimum, practical and, at best, resonate deeply with our target audiences.

It is important to keep in mind the previous stages that form the basis of our approach: being notable to the efforts as a whole, authentic in our messaging, trusted by the audiences and inclusive in our approach. Now is the time to be versatile in our execution and evolve with the changing dynamics of the campaign and its audiences.

We'll also explore the tools that can help you adapt to changing realities, the grassroots distribution strategies that can put your campaign directly in touch with the communities you aim to engage, and the short-term metrics that will help you measure your impact—because if you don't know your impact, you won't know when to adapt.

We'll also discuss how to keep your finger on the pulse of community response, ensuring that your strategies are resonant as well as effective—and ensuring that you're versatile enough to change if you need to as you plan and then launch your NX campaign.

The two stages of GO—Versatile and Evolving—are the most interconnected of all the stages of the NX experience, so it's helpful to keep a few things in mind to ensure we have the right context:

- In both these stages, metrics are our closest ally.
- Short-term metrics allow us to be Versatile, while mid- and long-term metrics allow us to Evolve.
- In our launch, Versatility helps us make our initial splash, using grassroots channels to introduce our campaign to our audiences and communities; Evolve takes us into a maintenance and evolution phase.
- Being Versatile means empowering our audiences and communities with the creative assets they need to generate content themselves as they see fit.

Prepare to Launch: Integrating Strategy and Creativity

An NX launch is not quite like a traditional campaign launch. We need to plan a launch that will transcend traditional marketing boundaries, intertwining creative vision, cultural foresight and an intimate understanding of your audience's landscape.

We need to refine our strategies to seamlessly incorporate stakeholder insights. That way, we can make sure every piece of the puzzle fits perfectly and resonates with the market we're aiming to capture while empowering our audiences with the content and creative assets to generate their own content.

Strategic Refinement

Before the grand reveal, revisit your strategy. Does it still echo the latest cultural nuances and market dynamics? If not, it's time to be Versatile. The process we described in the Trusted stage helped develop an intentionally flexible strategy that could adapt based on live insights from grassroots networks. If those insights have changed, tweak your communication tactics to ensure they still mirror your audience's current behaviours and preferences for a successful launch.

From Awareness to Action: Crafting Compelling Messages

The transition from capturing attention to spurring action is delicate. Your messaging at this stage isn't just about informing, it's about motivating. To ensure this, develop a series of steps to align your content with stakeholder and NX team expectations:

- Your communication and launch should bridge the gap between capturing attention and encouraging meaningful action.
- Do a final check to make sure your content was developed to live organically on platforms where your target communities naturally engage, fostering a natural progression from awareness to consideration.
- The purpose of your communication in this phase is to inspire action. Double-check that your content is informative and compelling.
- Develop a simple checklist to check against with your stakeholders and NX teams. For example:
  - Clear Calls-to-Action (CTAs): Whether it's 'Learn More', 'Join Now', or 'Share with Friends', ensure that each CTA is crystal clear and provides a direct pathway for engagement.
  - Highlight Benefits: Emphasise the value

of the action you're asking your audience to take. Why should they click, sign up, or participate? Articulate the benefits in a way that resonates with their cultural context and personal interests.

- Reduce Barriers to Action: Your audience is more likely to take action if the process is simple and user-friendly, such as a sign-up form that is concise, easy to fill and optimised for mobile devices.

Remember, your strategy should be as engaging as it is informative, ready to evolve based on feedback and impact assessments.

Prepare Campaign and Media Kits

Our campaign and media kits need to reflect the inclusivity of the co-creation process.

Campaign Kit: A comprehensive package containing campaign guidelines, individual in-language style guides, and creative outputs for client areas, community organisations and other stakeholders.

Media Kit: A ready-to-use package containing press releases, media contacts and other essential information to facilitate effective media relations.

Integrating Cultural Insights

Your strategy should respect and reflect the cultural nuances of your audience. The best way to ensure cultural appropriateness and buy-in is by involving your NX teams, ambassadors, people of influence and local teams in strategy development. For example, adapting marketing collateral to reflect local festivals or traditions can significantly increase engagement. It's important to offer remuneration when appropriate as it's a practical indication that you respect stakeholders' time and efforts.

Framework Agility: Adaptive Objectives

Your go-to-market plan should be as versatile as the market itself. Avoid setting yourself rigid goals. Instead, set objectives that adapt to market trends and community sentiments. For instance, stakeholder feedback might lead a campaign initially targeting brand awareness to pivot to community engagement.

Adaptability is crucial, allowing you to react promptly while keeping long-term goals in sight.

Prepare for Versatility

Versatility isn't just about being prepared to implement changes but being prepared to implement them at speed. Developing or gathering a dedicated rapid response team can address sudden shifts in market sentiment or other immediate needs.

- Be prepared to implement changes swiftly.
- Establish a team structure and communication plan that supports quick decision-making and execution.
- Include the NX Ambassadors.

Continuous Feedback Loop

Create a feedback loop to refine your strategy continually. Regularly adjust your approach based on performance data and stakeholder feedback.

- Plan for customer feedback methods in post-product launch to make adjustments in product features or marketing approach.
- Establish feedback loops and utilise community ambassadors for ongoing insights. This approach builds trust, ensures sustainable impact and optimises resource allocation.

As we gear up for the launch, it's crucial to stay alert and ready to engage with the unfolding dynamics of the market. Don't fall into the trap of thinking that the launch phase is just about putting plans into action. It's a critical period for learning in real time and responding swiftly to how the market and our audience interact with our campaign.

Launching a campaign in NX means being prepared

to take both proactive and reactive measures. It's a time to engage with the market and respond to audience feedback as it happens.

Soft launch: Test, Learn and Implement

If you have time and want more reassurance about your launch, consider a 'test and learn' approach in which you assess the effectiveness of pilot campaigns before a full-scale launch. This gives you a chance to tailor your messaging for different regions, platforms or subsets of audiences and evaluate the impact. Your strategy should accurately reflect cultural subtleties and nuances, backed up by cultural consultants or local teams if helpful. Maintain versatility in your implementation with a team structure that enables quick decision-making and action.

Launch

It's here! Time to launch. The thoughtful execution of your NX campaign takes you back to the work you did scoping out your strategy in the Trusted stage. Your strategies now will range from public relations endeavours to leveraging in-language media outlets and initiating grassroots movements.

The essence of the NX approach lies in the meticulous crafting of deliverables that are fundamental to the campaign's adaptability, efficacy and enduring influence. We need to meticulously delineate these critical deliverables to make them the structural pillars of our NX initiative. Additionally, we begin integrating immediate short-term metrics that will guide our versatility throughout the campaign's lifecycle.

Launching With Your Channels

As we enter the launch stage, the channels we've identified based on our audience personas play a pivotal role. We need to activate both digital and traditional channels in a coordinated effort in order to reach our audience effectively at the right place and time.

Strategic Launch on Selected Channels

Digital Platforms: Use platforms such as WhatsApp for a reach that can span local, grassroots communities all the way to global peers, especially if your target audience includes people who communicate with family overseas.

Traditional Media: It's often a mistake to overlook

the power of traditional media. Depending on your audience research, this might include community radio stations, regional newspapers, or even TV broadcasts.

Tailored Approach: Remember, the key is to tailor your launch strategy to the preferences of your audience segments. Younger demographics might be more engaged with an immersive digital campaign, while older groups may be more receptive to messages delivered through traditional media.

Practical Steps for Launching

Channel Coordination: Ensure that your messaging is consistent across all selected channels yet tailored to the unique format and audience of each.

Timing: Plan your launch to coincide with times when your audience is most active and receptive on your chosen channels. It might also be possible to align this with special community events or festivals.

Monitoring and Adjustment: As you roll out your campaign, closely monitor the performance across different channels. Be prepared to make real-time adjustments based on engagement and feedback. (We'll get deeper into short-term metrics soon.)

In this launch phase, our selection of channels is more than just finding a way to get our message 'out there'. It's a deliberate strategy to connect with our audience in spaces they trust and value. Our choices should embrace the nuances of cultural sensitivity and resonance, ensuring that our message reaches our audience and speaks to them meaningfully.

Remember, a successful launch is as much about how you communicate as it is about what you communicate. By carefully selecting and using your channels, you're poised to maximise your reach and ROI, truly connecting with the heart of your audience, whether it's through digital or traditional channels or PR.

A multifaceted, comprehensive approach ensures a robust launch, combining the extensive reach of digital platforms with the depth and personal touch of grassroots initiatives.

Launching With Community

In NX marketing, grassroots distribution becomes a core strategy to achieve genuine engagement by interacting in a community's own cultural spaces via their preferred communication methods.

While digital platforms and mainstream media have their place, nothing replaces the authenticity of grassroots initiatives in reaching audiences in their native language on native devices and through channels that they use every day.

Grassroots Distribution: A Case for Community-centric Implementation

Grassroots distribution is the epitome of versatility in action. It encourages feedback from audiences, so it allows for real-time adjustments. Whether it's distributing flyers at a local cultural event, partnering with community and target organisations for workshops, or leveraging local influencers to amplify your message, grassroots efforts take your message to the heart of the community.

The NX Ambassador Team plays a vital role in this strategy. With their close connection to the ground and direct involvement with various stakeholders, they serve as the campaign's pulse. Their insights are invaluable for adapting strategies in response to community feedback, ensuring the campaign remains resonant, relevant and culturally attuned.

The benefits are manifold:

Immediate Feedback: Grassroots initiatives allow for real-time interaction with your target audience, providing invaluable insights that can be used to adjust your campaign on the fly.

Cultural Sensitivity: By engaging directly with the community, you're better positioned to understand the cultural nuances that can make or break your campaign.

Enhanced Credibility: Community members are more likely to trust information that comes from within their own circles, enhancing the credibility of your campaign.

Cost-Effectiveness: While it is definitely not always the case, grassroots initiatives often have the potential to be more cost-effective than large-scale media buys, especially when well-planned and executed.

Community Empowerment: Perhaps most importantly, grassroots distribution empowers the community by involving them in the campaign, turning passive recipients into active participants.

In the implementation phase, grassroots distribution is one of our most versatile tools. It will enable us to adapt, listen and pivot, ensuring that our campaigns are disseminated among and embraced by the communities we aim to serve.

Provide Tools for User Generated Content (UGC)

Another vital tool in this phase is User Generated Content. If you empower a community with a set of campaign materials, guidelines for how to use them, and direct contact with your NX Ambassador Team, they can generate content that truly reflects their communities week by week. That helps turn them from your audience into your advocates.

The materials you provide could range from informational brochures and digital assets to more interactive elements such as training sessions. The aim is to equip individuals with the knowledge and tools they need to effectively spread the message within their own circles and generate their own content, taking resonance and targeted messaging to a whole new level.

Adapting to Community Feedback

Whether it's through community forums, social media interactions, or direct conversations, feedback from grassroots initiatives is a gold mine for long-term adaptation.

> **Feedback Loops:** Establish mechanisms for continuous feedback collection, such as recurring community surveys or regular focus group discussions.

Community Ambassadors: Utilise community leaders or influencers as ambassadors who can provide ongoing insights into community sentiments.

Long-Term Benefits

Community Trust: Consistent and adaptive grassroots engagement builds trust, turning your target audience from recipients to active participants.

Sustainable Impact: Grassroots initiatives that evolve based on community feedback are more likely to have a sustainable impact as they remain relevant to the community's changing needs.

Resource Optimisation: Long-term engagement allows for more effective resource allocation as you gain a deeper understanding of what truly resonates with your community.

By understanding the life cycle of grassroots initiatives and the importance of long-term adaptation, you're launching a campaign and building a community. And in the world of NX, that is the ultimate goal.

Short-term Metrics: Components of Impactful Reporting

As we go to market, the need for a robust monitoring and metrics system becomes paramount. A versatile campaign makes informed and strategic adjustments for continuous improvement. Short-term metrics are crucial in telling us how to adapt and pivot, providing immediate insights into the effectiveness of our strategies.

I've listed here the type of key performance indicators (KPIs) you might set in order to ensure that your initiatives remain versatile immediately after you launch and to figure out how they might need to change.

Example Short-term KPI	Description
Real-time Analytics	Utilise real-time analytics tools to track key performance indicators as the campaign unfolds.
Community Feedback	Continuously gather and analyse qualitative feedback from community interactions to provide context to metrics.
Audience size	Confirm that the campaign is reaching the intended audience size shortly after launch.
Impressions	Monitor the number of impressions generated, ensuring they align with the campaign's target demographic.
Click-through rates (CTR)	Assess how effectively your content prompts action by tracking CTR and making immediate adjustments

Example Short-term KPI	Description
Engagement rates	Monitor engagement rates to gauge interaction with your campaign materials and tailor calls-to-action accordingly.
Time spent on content	Measure the time users spend consuming your content, adjusting content types or formats based on performance.
Community engagement levels	Track community engagement levels to ensure the campaign fosters active interaction within the target audience.
Click-through Rate (CTR) by Channel	Measure CTR on different marketing channels to identify which ones are driving immediate engagement.
Bounce Rate	Assess the bounce rate of campaign-specific pages to determine how well they retain visitors and encourage interaction.
Social Shares and Mentions	Count social shares and mentions related to your campaign content to measure its virality within the short term.
Lead Generation Metrics	Monitor metrics like the number of leads captured, form submissions, or downloads of lead magnets in the short term.
Event Registrations	Measure the number of registrations or RSVPs received shortly after promoting events in the campaign.
App Downloads	Track the number of app downloads and installations resulting from the campaign in the short term.
Email Open Rate	Assess how many recipients engage with your email content by monitoring the open rate in the short term.
User-generated Content (UGC)	Measure the volume of user-generated content related to your campaign, such as reviews or social media posts.

Monitoring Performance

This list is not exhaustive, but it will give you a good idea of the type of metrics that can inform any decision to update your strategy. As you use tools like sentiment analysis and social listening for up-to-the-minute community feedback, adjusting strategies as needed, you can also engage in scenario planning for different market conditions, crafting multiple strategy pathways to accommodate changes such as shifts in consumer behaviour or new market entrants.

Your strategy will be informed by metrics from two main sources:

Real-time Analytics: Utilising real-time KPIs to monitor key performance indicators.

Community Feedback: Active collection and analysis of qualitative feedback from community interactions to provide context to your quantitative metrics.

Remember that the success of any action-driven campaign is inextricably linked to the platform on which it is executed. No one would announce a community fair on a niche podcast. In the same way, NX campaigns need to consider:

Frequency of Interaction: Are the platforms frequented regularly by the target community?

Nature of Interaction: Some platforms are better suited for passive consumption, while others foster active engagement. Tailor the campaign's call-to-action based on the nature of the chosen platform.

Best Practices

What and how often you report is up to you. This is more art than science, but the purpose of whatever process you adopt should be not to miss something that would require a change in your campaign strategy.

Frequency: Determine the frequency of your reports based on the campaign's needs and stakeholder's expectations. It might be weekly, monthly, or quarterly.

Customisation: Tailor the reports to meet the specific needs and interests of different stakeholder groups.

Accessibility: Ensure that reports are easily accessible, which might be through digital dashboards, PDFs, or physical copies. Some stakeholders may be happier with one format than another.

Review and Feedback: Create opportunities for stakeholders to review the report and provide feedback, further enhancing the campaign's versatility.

By embracing impactful reporting, you maintain the pulse of your current campaign and lay the groundwork for future successes. Reporting like this isn't just a back-end task, as in traditional campaigns, but a strategic tool that will amplify the versatility and impact of your NX efforts and lay the foundations for ongoing management.

The basis of all analysis of a campaign is reliable data. That data can be reported in a number of ways. Depending on your particular situation, some of these are usually the most helpful:

Executive Summary: A high-level overview that captures key achievements, challenges and next steps.

KPI Analysis: A deep dive into KPIs, measured against the benchmarks.

Community Feedback: A summary of qualitative feedback collected from the community, providing context to the quantitative metrics.

Financial Metrics: An analysis of the campaign's ROI, customer acquisition costs and other financial metrics that gauge effectiveness.

Recommendations and Future Steps: Based on the data and insights collected, a section outlining recommended adjustments and future strategies.

Versatility in NX means being agile enough to pivot when necessary and proactive enough to anticipate shifts in cultural norms and market trends. This duality requires a keen sense of awareness and continuously adjusting your campaign to reflect evolving objectives based on short-term metrics such as KPIs. As we get deeper into the campaign, it's time to shift our focus from its immediate impact to its continued success. For that stage—which we call Evolving—we need to be more aware of mid- and long-term metrics.

In the next chapter, we'll see how we can measure our campaign's ongoing impact and how it might help shape better campaigns in the future.

Recap

- Execution in NX is synonymous with versatility. Although this phase is about the launch, it's also about being agile and responsive to the audience's evolving needs and preferences.
- It's a dynamic process of adapting your strategy to real-time feedback and shifting market dynamics. It's an ongoing dialogue with your audience, a dance of adaptability and responsiveness.
- Be prepared to adapt your strategy based on real-time feedback and changing market dynamics.

CHAPTER 7

Be Evolving

'What's very dangerous is to not evolve.'
—JEFF BEZOS, Founder, Amazon

IN THE LAST CHAPTER, we talked about the immediacy of launching and measuring short-term metrics in campaigns. Now, we move on to a critical final stage—sustaining and adapting our efforts for long-term impact.

The final stage of Native Experience (NX) Marketing, Evolving, is guided by the business philosophy known as Kaizen (see author's note), in which the principles of incremental progress and sustained growth are embedded at the heart of our approach. A commitment to Kaizen ensures that every aspect of our strategy is consistently advancing towards excellence—and toward the Notable status we set out to reach at the beginning of our NX journey. Evolution is about fostering a culture that embraces change and actively seeks it out to enhance our performance systematically.

The landscape of NX is so fluid that the only constant is change itself, whether it's the ebb and flow of cultural trends, the shifting demographics of target communities, or the unpredictable turns of global events. The need for continuous tweaking and improvement is essential to give your NX efforts a lasting impact.

As we navigate the complexities of sustaining and adapting our NX, let's embrace the evolving nature of our work, our communities, our audiences and, indeed, the world itself.

We'll see how evolving a campaign post-launch is a question of both art and science.

> ***Author's note:*** *Kaizen is a business philosophy that originated in Japan after World War II, meaning 'change for the better' or 'continuous improvement'. This concept played a crucial role in Japan's post-war recovery and economic growth. Essentially, Kaizen suggests that small, consistent positive changes can lead to significant improvements. It requires every level of an organisation to work together to achieve incremental progress by, say, refining processes, improving customer service or enhancing manufacturing efficiency.*
>
> *Kaizen originated in the Japanese manufacturing*

> *industry, but it has spread to influence practices in organisations worldwide. It is less a series of actions than a mindset that promotes team and stakeholder participation in innovation and efficiency, cultivating a proactive culture of growth and learning.*
>
> *The ultimate goal of NX Marketing is to produce communications that resonate across cultural boundaries, and the Kaizen philosophy helps teams to seek out and implement gradual improvements in their efforts. By adopting the Kaizen mindset, NX Teams can ensure that their strategies are not static but are continually refined in response to feedback and changing market dynamics, embodying the adaptable and progressive spirit at the core of NX.*

The Evolving stage is where you see the tangible results of your efforts. While the key performance indicators may vary depending on your specific objectives, they should always be culturally relevant. Whether it's making a purchase, signing up for a service, or participating in a community event, the conversion metrics should reflect the values and behaviours of the cultural groups you are targeting.

As the final stage of the GO phase, Evolving shifts the focus from building interest and engagement to achieving tangible, measurable outcomes. In the realm of NX, conversion isn't as simple as a transaction or a click; it's a meaningful interaction that fulfils the campaign's primary objectives while fostering deeper community relationships.

Aligning Goals and Metrics

Conversion, which is traditionally associated with sales or sign-ups, takes on a more nuanced meaning within NX communities. Here, it signifies a genuine alignment of interests between an organisation and a cultural group. Whether it's adopting a new practice, showing up for a community event, or spreading a crucial message, conversion reflects a deeper engagement and commitment.

Primary and Secondary Conversion Goals

Because NX campaigns and initiatives are so diverse, it's essential to identify both primary and secondary conversion goals for your specific campaign. This ensures a multi-dimensional approach to gauging what success means to you.

> **Primary Goals**: These are the foremost objectives of the campaign. They represent the most urgent and impactful outcomes you aim to achieve. Primary goals might, for example, focus on direct conversions such as sales, sign-ups, or other forms of commitment that bring immediate value to your efforts.

Secondary Goals: Secondary goals encompass softer metrics, such as brand awareness, customer engagement, or sentiment change among your target audience. They often serve as stepping stones toward achieving the primary objectives, but they may also provide additional value that complements the main goals. While they may not command the spotlight, secondary goals are vital to a campaign's overall success.

Metrics that Matter

As we saw in the last chapter, we analyse the GO phase with short-term metrics. These are the immediate KPIs, such as click-through rates or initial engagement levels, which are crucial during the launch phase. As we move into the Evolving stage, two other types of metrics become more important:

Mid-term Metrics: As your campaign gains traction, focus on metrics like customer retention rates and community engagement levels to gauge ongoing impact.

Long-term Metrics: These are the metrics that truly measure the sustainability of your campaign, such as lifetime customer value or long-term community impact.

Here's an example of how aligning your goals and metrics might look:

	Mid-term Metrics	**Long-term Metrics**
Primary Goals	**Conversion Rates:** Monitor the percentage of the target audience taking the desired actions, such as making a purchase or signing up for campaign-specific offerings.	**Customer Retention Rates:** Track how well the campaign retains customers acquired. This will help measure the campaign's impact on long-term customer loyalty.
	Return on Investment (ROI): Calculate the financial return on your investments, comparing it to the overall campaign cost. This will help you gauge the immediate financial impact.	**Net Promoter Scores (NPS):** Continuously gauge customer loyalty and satisfaction by measuring NPS scores. This will provide insights into the campaign's lasting effect on customer sentiment.
	Customer Acquisition Costs: Assess the cost associated with acquiring a new customer through the campaign, focusing on the efficiency of your acquisition strategies.	**Community Engagement Levels:** Assess the level of ongoing interaction within the communities involved in your campaign. Monitor metrics such as participation rates, user-generated content and community growth.

	Mid-term Metrics	**Long-term Metrics**
Secondary Goals	**Brand Awareness:** Track metrics like brand mentions, social media reach and website traffic to gauge the increase in brand visibility resulting from the campaign.	**Social Media Community Growth:** This metric tracks the expansion of your social media community, including the increase in followers, subscribers and community members who engage with your content and brand over the long term.
	Customer Engagement: Monitor customer engagement through metrics such as click-through rates, social media interactions and email open rates.	**Content Engagement Over Time:** Content engagement metrics assess how effectively your campaign content continues to resonate with your audience over an extended period. It measures sustained interest and interaction with your campaign materials.
	Sentiment Analysis: Use sentiment analysis tools to measure changes in the sentiment of your target audience towards your brand or campaign messages.	**Sentiment Consistency:** Sentiment consistency evaluates whether the positive sentiment generated during your campaign is maintained over the long term. It measures the durability of positive perceptions and emotions associated with your brand or message.

Strategies for Higher Conversion Rates

Achieving a successful conversion in any campaign requires a combination of trust-building, clear communication and cultural sensitivity. In the NX Experience, they're all amplified. Here are some strategies to enhance conversion rates:

Tailored Messaging: Go beyond generic messages to speak directly to the unique needs and concerns of your target audience. This involves highlighting specific benefits, dispelling common misconceptions and addressing particular concerns that resonate with the demographic you aim to reach.

Use of Testimonials and Stories: People resonate with real-life stories. Incorporating testimonials or narrative elements into your campaign can build trust and inspire action. These stories should ideally come from individuals within the community who have already taken the desired action, thereby serving as relatable role models for prospective converts.

Leverage Community Influencers: Collaborating with trusted community leaders or influencers can amplify a campaign's reach and credibility, driving higher conversions.

Create Easy Pathways to Convert: Simplicity is key when it comes to conversion. Ensure that the process for taking the desired action is straightforward and easily accessible. This could mean providing clear instructions, reducing the number of steps involved, or offering multiple channels through which the action can be taken.

Feedback and Iteration: Regularly gauge the effectiveness of conversion strategies. Collect feedback, understand barriers and adjust tactics accordingly.

Evolving encapsulates the process of transforming passive recipients into active advocates. It's one thing to acquire a customer or participant, but it's another to inspire individuals to become champions of your cause within communities. In many communities, ties are strong, and word-of-mouth plays a critical role in spreading information. As such, engagement is pivotal in driving a lasting, widespread impact.

Evolution focuses on nurturing long-term relationships with your newly converted customers or participants. By encouraging advocates to share their positive experiences, you retain their loyalty and leverage their influence within their communities to amplify your message.

Post-Conversion Engagement

While many marketing strategies prioritise conversion, NX efforts prioritise post-conversion engagement. Within tight-knit communities, personal experiences and narratives can significantly shape group perceptions. Nurturing relationships after conversion:

- Solidifies trust, ensuring long-term loyalty.

- Lays the groundwork for future campaigns, providing a receptive audience base.

Strategies for Advocacy Within Communities

Turning converted customers or participants into advocates requires a blend of continuous engagement, acknowledgment and value addition:

Celebrate Success Stories: Publicly acknowledge and share personal stories of individuals who have had positive experiences after taking the desired action. These testimonials serve multiple purposes: they validate the campaign and debunk myths, as well as alleviate concerns that potential converts may have.

Facilitate Community Dialogues: Create spaces—in the shape of community forums, virtual chats, or town hall meetings—where people can openly discuss their experiences, ask questions and share insights.

Acknowledge and Reward Advocacy: Active advocacy should be acknowledged and rewarded. Recognition can take various forms, from social media shout-outs and certificates to small tokens of appreciation—such gestures motivate advocates and encourage others to take similar actions.

Encouraging the Cascading Effect

The ultimate aim of our Evolving stage is to stimulate an effect in which your campaign 'cascades' throughout your audience group:

>   **Individual Experiences:** Start by ensuring that every individual's experience with the campaign is positive, memorable and meaningful.
>
>   **Community Conversations:** As individuals share their stories, it sparks dialogues, leading to a broader community discussion. Positive testimonials can influence group sentiment, slowly shifting perceptions.
>
>   **Community-wide Acceptance:** As more individuals advocate and the narrative becomes predominantly positive, there's a gradual shift towards community-wide acceptance and endorsement.

Here we aim to go beyond interaction. It's about fostering deep-rooted relationships, turning individuals into ambassadors and then leveraging their advocacy to achieve a domino effect of positive influence and acceptance within a target community—even one where the first reaction to a campaign might have been somewhat resistant.

Mid-term Metrics: Ongoing Management

Ongoing management is not about maintaining the status quo but constant refinement. It's about keeping your finger on the pulse of community sentiment, market trends and performance metrics and making informed adjustments accordingly. Changes or events that have little or no impact on some communities may have a huge impact on others, requiring that you evolve your campaign. This is where your NX Ambassador Team becomes invaluable, serving as your eyes and ears on the ground, providing real-time insights that can inform strategic decisions. Those decisions are also informed by three other components:

Regular Reporting: Periodic reports that provide a comprehensive overview of the campaign's impact and effectiveness.

Stakeholder Updates: Regular briefings or newsletters to keep all stakeholders informed and engaged throughout the campaign.

Post-campaign Review: A thorough analysis of the campaign's performance, including lessons learned and recommendations for future initiatives.

Key Components of Ongoing Management

As in other elements of the NX Framework, ongoing management requires remaining alert to the real-time situation and being prepared to adapt if necessary. These are some of the key tools you can use:

Performance Audits: Regularly review key performance indicators to assess the effectiveness of your campaign strategies. This is not a one-off task but a recurring activity that ensures your campaign remains aligned with its objectives.

Community Engagement: Keep the lines of communication open with your target communities. Use social media, community forums and grassroots initiatives to gather ongoing feedback.

Stakeholder Communication: Maintain an open dialogue with internal and external stakeholders. Regular updates keep everyone on the same page and provide opportunities for collaborative problem-solving.

Resource Allocation: As the campaign progresses, you may need to reallocate resources—be it budget, manpower, or time—to areas that require more attention or have proven to be more effective.

Contingency Planning: Always have a Plan B (and C and D). As we saw in the last chapter, the ability to pivot is crucial in a dynamic market environment, and having contingency plans in place ensures you're prepared for any eventualities.

Adapting to Cultural Dynamics and Demographic Shifts

In a world where cultural norms and demographics are ever-changing, the ability to adapt is a necessity. In general, the key is to be aware of changes and shifts in community sentiment, but there are a handful of tools that make the process easier:

Cultural Calendars: Keep an eye on cultural holidays, events and shifts that could impact your campaign. Adapt your messaging and tactics accordingly.

Demographic Data: Regularly update your demographic data to ensure that your campaign remains aligned with the evolving makeup of your target communities.

Trend Analysis: Utilise tools and platforms that can help you identify emerging trends in real time, allowing for proactive adjustments to your campaign strategies.

Mid-term Metrics: Feedback Loops

In the NX framework, feedback is vital. It's the lifeblood of the entire approach, providing real-time insights that can be used to refine strategies, adjust tactics and enhance community engagement. But collecting feedback is only half the equation; the other half is creating effective feedback loops that facilitate ongoing dialogue with your stakeholders and target communities in the mid-term.

Methods for Collecting Feedback

The nature of the feedback you collect will depend on many factors, including the communities you engage with, the nature of the campaign, and where you are in the campaign chronologically. The key is to find the feedback that most helps you for the duration of the campaign, enabling you to evolve it as needed.

Surveys and Questionnaires: Deploy short, culturally sensitive surveys across various channels to gauge community sentiment. After the initial launch, continue to deploy surveys to gauge the evolving sentiments of your target communities.

Social Media Monitoring and Polls: Use social listening tools to track mentions, hashtags and conversations related to your campaign. Utilise social media platforms to run quick polls, offering a real-time pulse on community sentiment.

Community Forums: Host community forums or focus groups, either online or in-person, to gather in-depth qualitative insights. Integrate qualitative feedback from community interactions, both online and through grassroots initiatives, to provide context to your quantitative metrics.

Stakeholder Interviews: Conduct one-on-one interviews with key stakeholders to understand their perspectives and concerns. Regularly schedule reviews with internal and external stakeholders to gather their insights on campaign performance and community reception.

Grassroots Interactions: Leverage your grassroots distribution channels to collect feedback directly from the community.

Real-time Monitoring: Utilise real-time analytics tools to keep a pulse on your campaign's performance, allowing for immediate adjustments.

Alignment Checks: Regularly revisit the insights and discoveries from earlier phases to ensure that your KPIs and tactics remain aligned with your initial objectives.

Adaptive Learning: Use the data collected to adjust the current campaign and inform future strategies, making each campaign an opportunity for organisational learning.

Consistent and comprehensive reporting keeps stakeholders informed and provides a structured opportunity for strategic reassessment.

Utilising Feedback for Evolution
Feedback loops are the cornerstone of a versatile campaign. They allow you to adapt to market trends and the evolving sentiments and needs of your target communities. By actively seeking, analysing and acting upon feedback, you're optimising your current campaign and investing in the long-term success of all your NX Marketing efforts.

FEEDBACK FUELS CAMPAIGN EVOLUTION

The feedback you receive on a campaign via your reporting processes becomes a resource for adjusting your campaign in real-time.

Archive all feedback and related adjustments for future reference to create a knowledge base that can inform future NX Marketing initiatives.

Long-term Metrics: Beyond Immediate KPIs

While immediate KPIs offer valuable insights into the initial success of a campaign, they only tell part of the story. During the Evolving stage of the NX framework, we also need to shift our focus to long-term metrics that provide a more comprehensive view of a campaign's impact and adaptability.

Adapting Strategies Based on Long-term Metrics

> **Data-driven Adaptation:** Utilise long-term metrics to identify areas for strategic adaptation. For example, if customer retention rates are declining, it may be time to refresh your community engagement strategies.

Benchmarking: Regularly compare your long-term metrics against industry benchmarks or past campaigns to gauge your campaign's relative success and areas for improvement.

Why Long-term Metrics Matter

Strategic Adaptation: Long-term metrics provide the data needed for ongoing strategic adjustments, ensuring your campaign remains effective and relevant.

Sustainable Impact: A focus on long-term metrics ensures that you're making a splash and creating ripples that have a lasting impact.

Stakeholder Confidence: Demonstrating success through long-term metrics can build stakeholder confidence, securing support for future initiatives.

Focusing on long-term metrics helps to measure your campaign's success and sets the stage for ongoing evolution and long-term impact. It's not enough to just start strong; what really matters is how well you can adapt and sustain your efforts over time.

> ***Author's note:*** *While immediate campaign success is often the spotlight, the Evolving stage of the NX framework urges us to look beyond the present by aligning stakeholders for long-term strategic shifts, which can also help us lay the groundwork for future campaigns. We can ensure that all stakeholders share a common vision through regular communication and updates, strategic workshops and feedback channels that allow stakeholders to give insights that are incorporated into decision-making. Making sure that stakeholders are aligned will keep everyone on the same page with regard to our priorities, which helps in effective resource allocation for future campaigns and ensures that aligned stakeholders are more likely to support necessary strategic shifts in the future, even if they involve short-term risks, in order to achieve long-term gains. Often, stakeholders become deeply involved in their personal experience of a campaign and their interactions within their own community, celebrating the 'wins' that come with success and enjoying any awards and tokens of recognition, such as being featured in local media.*

Reporting and Refining

Without regular, insightful reporting, it's difficult, if not impossible, to evolve your NX efforts, both for the current campaign and for campaigns in the future. Reporting serves multiple purposes: it measures the impact and effectiveness of your strategies and provides a structured framework for stakeholder communication, strategic reassessment and future planning.

Reporting lays the foundation for your long-term success and evolution in four main ways:

Accountability: Regular reporting holds all parties accountable, ensuring that objectives are set and rigorously pursued and measured.

Transparency: Detailed reports foster transparency, providing stakeholders with a clear view of what's working, what's not, and why.

Decision-making: Data-driven reports offer actionable insights that can inform real-time decision-making, enhancing the campaign's versatility.

Long-term Strategy: Periodic reporting creates a historical record that can be invaluable for future NX Marketing initiatives.

Refining Tactics and Strategies

Your mid- and long-term metrics—both performance data and feedback from the communities involved in the campaign—are the basis for you to be able to refine your marketing tactics and strategies. This is where the

Evolving aspect of the NX framework truly comes into its own. It allows you to make data-driven adjustments during the life of the campaign, thanks to the flexibility you've built into your strategy throughout.

Using techniques such as A/B testing of different messaging strategies within your target communities, studying performance metrics of different elements of your campaign and listening to qualitative feedback from the community, you can highlight more or less successful elements of your campaign and adapt them accordingly.

Future Campaign Planning

No NX campaign exists in isolation. Each successful campaign is a stepping stone to the next, as you take your knowledge of communities and the links you have developed within them by using NX ambassadors—not to mention any lessons you've learned about strategy and operation—and use them as the foundation for whatever campaigns might come next. This process will, to some extent, happen organically throughout your campaigns, but it will be more effective if you make a conscious commitment to following a series of simple steps:

- **Post-campaign Reviews:** Conduct thorough post-campaign reviews that assess the success

of the current campaign and extract lessons for future initiatives.
- **Knowledge Repository:** Create a repository of campaign data, stakeholder feedback and other insights that can serve as a valuable resource for future campaign planning.
- **Pilot Programs:** Consider running small-scale pilot programs to test new strategies or technologies, using them as a stepping stone for future large-scale campaigns.

Into the Future

By continuing to resonate and evolve, your campaign will have a lasting influence that will benefit any future initiatives by creating an institutional memory and improving your long-term capabilities. By having stakeholders aligned with your long-term objectives, you ensure that your strategic efforts become part of a continuum within communities. Each future campaign will be able to draw on a legacy of impactful community engagement that leading individuals within the community have experienced in a positive way. To some extent, you're preaching to the choir—which is a great foundation for any campaign.

In that way, the Evolving stage of an NX campaign

has no 'end'. It continues to resonate within individuals, communities and your own organisation. As we saw at the start of the chapter, Evolving draws deeply on the philosophy of Kaizen: a constant stream of small improvements rather than spectacular breakthroughs and innovations.

This is where you'll discover the lasting strength of a carefully constructed NX experience. It doesn't simply promote the service or product that's the subject of the individual campaign. It helps create an environment in which NX design becomes innate in every campaign as marketing organisations become increasingly familiar with operating in the only way that acknowledges and celebrates the rich cultural mosaic of the contemporary world—and the only way that future campaigns will succeed: the NX Experience.

Recap

- The Evolving stage is about embedding incremental progress and sustained growth at the heart of our operations, based on the Kaizen philosophy.
- Our campaign should seek tangible outcomes in the shape of individual transactions and meaningful interactions that foster ongoing community relationships and loyalty.
- We leverage our audience through engagement that turns passive recipients of our messaging into active advocates within our audience community.
- We track the ongoing effectiveness of our campaign by using both mid-term and long-term metrics.
- A system of ongoing management based on feedback loops from NX Ambassadors and audience groups allows us to evolve our messaging and points to possible directions for long-term strategy and future campaigns.

Be NATIVE

CONGRATULATIONS! IF YOU'VE WORKED through the stages outlined in this book, then you've used the NATIVE framework to conceive, create and launch an NX campaign that both acknowledges and benefits from the diverse communities that make up the market for your brand.

If you've not put the framework into action yet, then you have all the steps and tools you need to go ahead and tailor your campaigns to the people you want to receive your message.

It was a lot of work, but the rewards more than made up for the effort.

It's not time to relax, however. One of the underlying principles of NX Marketing is that it has to be dynamic because the community landscape in which you're operating is always fluid, never stationary.

If your marketplace doesn't stand still, neither can you.

NX Accountability: A Holistic Audit for Continuous Improvement

One way to ensure that you're constantly keeping up with change is through a cycle of campaign management. NX Accountability is not an endpoint but a continuous process. While it's crucial to focus on metrics like ROI and engagement rates, the NX Accountability approach broadens the scope of the feedback you receive to include cultural and representational factors that could influence your campaign's success over the long term.

This more holistic approach to accountability serves as a barometer for performance, authenticity, and inclusion.

It's worth constantly reviewing your campaigns with a view to both fine-tuning running campaigns and ensuring that you'll improve on future campaigns.

> **How Representative Were Your NX Teams?** A truly NX Marketing campaign begins with a representative team. From strategists to creatives, does your internal NX team reflect the diversity of the audience you're currently trying to reach?
>
> **Action Step:** Conduct a diversity audit of your team and identify areas for improvement. The more perspectives you can incorporate at the planning

stage, the more authentic and resonant your campaigns will be.

How Accurately Did Your Initiatives Represent Your Audiences? It's not just about numbers; it's about resonance. Did your campaign imagery, messaging and channels align with the cultural nuances and preferences of your target audience?

Action Step: Compare initial audience research to post-campaign surveys or NX Voice Forum results. Identify gaps and misalignments that might have affected the campaign's effectiveness.

Post-campaign Reflection. An overall audit should extend beyond the specific campaign to consider the brand's broader impact. What are the lessons learned, and how can they be applied to future initiatives?

Action Step: Conduct a comprehensive post-mortem meeting that addresses both successes and areas for growth.

An NX Accountability approach makes room for nuanced evaluations that look outside numbers to achieve a deep understanding of your NX efforts. That enables you to align your internal teams accordingly, ensuring that your initiatives truly resonate with your intended audience.

Join a Movement

We started this book with the fact that more than 7,100 languages are spoken around the world, and hundreds across Australia, Canada, the UK and USA. As we've seen, however, diversity doesn't have to be an obstacle for marketers and professionals who want their message to reach those communities who don't speak the majority language. Quite the opposite. Diversity can be a huge opportunity. It gives us a chance to tailor our messages, embrace cultural nuance, and find new audiences traditional campaigns don't reach. That gives us a commercial edge over our competitors, enables us to build brand loyalty within specific sections of the market, builds social cohesion and encourages deep understanding and appreciation of other cultures that can, in turn, influence the evolution of our products and services.

NX Marketing is a highly effective way to turn diversity from an obstacle into an opportunity. Armed with the information we've followed in this book, you're well set to take your own steps toward creating truly NX campaigns. However, if you'd like further guidance with your NX journey then feel free to get in touch.

The NX framework is not a tickbox exercise. It's a mindset, a commitment to continuous improvement and long-term impact. Standing still is not an option. The communities we engage with are continuously evolving, representing a dynamic blend of culture, sentiment and varying needs. Our strategies must be equally dynamic.

As someone who has navigated the complexities of NX efforts for years, I can attest to their power. NX is about building relationships that stand the test of time, creating a legacy and strategies that adapt to the ever-changing cultural environment and campaigns that resonate today and pave the way for future successes.

It's a commitment to learning, adapting and growing, ensuring that your NX efforts create a lasting impact. Embrace the change, adapt and evolve. Your future self—and your future campaigns—will thank you for it.

You're about to join a movement that is changing the face of modern marketing and bringing it in line with a rich, diverse, fascinating and exciting world in which opportunity is equal for all and no one is excluded.

Get ready to jump in and play your part!

Explore the latest in Native Experience Marketing at lexigo.com/nx

Work with Me

THE THRILL I FIND in the journey of native language communication and cross-cultural exchange is immeasurable. It's astonishing how much impact can be derived from what appears to be a simple concept: the power of language in building meaningful connections.

For me, there's a unique excitement in being present during those moments when marketing and communication teams suddenly 'get it'. That's when they understand what they used to perceive as foreign and ethnic is simply native to their audience and grasp how to harness that understanding for authentic and resonant communication results. Witnessing these lightbulb moments—where an organisation or brand's future shines brightly in its in-language communication—fills me with both purpose and delight.

The ethos of LEXIGO is based on this enthusiasm. As a professional translation and native language communications agency, we work tirelessly with organisations from the business and enterprise sectors to non-profit, government and public sector organisations. Our aim? To enable you to connect authentically and effectively with seamless native language communication between languages and cultures.

We focus on integrating strategic insights that are culturally nuanced and based on data.

In our strategic planning engagements, the process is not a monologue but a dialogue. Through the NX framework, I co-design a facilitation methodology that is tailored to your unique organisational circumstances and people. The objective isn't to impose a one-size-fits-all solution but rather to create a dynamic space where your team can collectively unearth solutions to your in-language, in-culture efforts. Through a blend of analytical tools and narrative discussions, we enable teams to explore, innovate and arrive at actionable NX strategies.

In each interaction, whether it's a planning session or a workshop, the goal remains the same: To help you and your teams experience your own 'native-first thinking' moments. Moments where the walls between 'us' and 'them' dissolve, and the expansive possibilities of a NATIVE approach to communication and marketing become vividly clear.

Work with me, and let's unlock those audience-first insights that can make your strategy powerful and culturally resonant.

You can contact me by

Emailing:
- nx@lexigo.com

Connecting or following me on LinkedIn:
- www.linkedin.com/in/mark-saba/

Or through the LEXIGO website:
- www.lexigo.com

Acknowledgements

IN THE EVOLUTION OF every concept, framework, or book, there are key individuals whose contributions breathe life into ideas and words. My journey in developing and articulating the Native Experience (NX) framework has been no different.

Our stories often start in the comfort of our homes, where we are nurtured by those who know us best. In my case, this sanctuary of learning and questioning was richly cultivated by both of my parents. My mother, Janet, an exceptional woman in the field of linguistics and translation, ignited my fascination with languages and the diversity of human communication. My father, Mark Snr., on the other hand, expanded my horizons through his profound interest in the arts, health, medicine and science.

My sister, Mimi, and brother, Joe, who never hesitated to tell me 'how it is', provided a grounding influence and a perspective only a sibling can give that taught me the importance of honesty and clarity, both in personal interactions and professional endeavours.

These dual influences have shaped the intellectual facets of my being and the multidisciplinary approach that underpins the NX framework.

I'd like to thank numerous others for their contributions:

The LEXIGO team, I am continually inspired by your dedication, creativity and innovation. Each and every one of you adds something special to our company culture, weaving together our NATIVE values and a shared vision that propels us forward. Your collective commitment is the keystone of our success, and it is because of you that we continue to grow and create opportunities. This book is a dedication to the journey we share and the stories we are yet to write together.

Brian Kane, host of LEXIGO's *The Native Experience Podcast*. Apart from bringing his passion, energy and curiosity to the show, Brian skillfully encourages individuals to share their NX stories, enriching our understanding and appreciation of perspectives and experiences.

To each guest of the Native Experience Podcast whose generosity in sharing time and insights brings to life the authentic and diverse stories of the Native Experience, enriching our framework with their invaluable perspectives and knowledge. Thank you.

Thank you to Cynthia Dearin, who has been there from LEXIGO's early days, nurturing its growth and my authorial aspirations. On the other side of the world, Andrzej Nedoma lent his strategic brilliance and belief in LEXIGO.

For her dedication and application of her community services expertise, thank you, Julie El Khoury, for bringing social impact initiatives into the fold at LEXIGO.

Lisa Tribuzio has a knack for making the invisible visible, giving voice to the often unheard and providing important insight into working with communities and diverse individuals.

Zaina Nasser has been an excellent editorial sounding board, especially for my marketing rambles.

Sophia Dickinson transitioned from a client to a cherished team member and friend, enriching our NX narrative.

Tony Lee has been a long-standing work partner; our synergy has grown, and I look forward to what's next.

Thanks to our endless linguistic discussions, Dr Erika Gonzales has been a catalyst for intellectual stimulation.

Special mention to Renato Beninatto, who offered wisdom when I was just stepping into the world of translation at the age of 20 and remains a guiding force that continues to inspire many across the industry. I also extend my deepest gratitude to Nataly Kelly, Josef Kubovský, Andrzej Nedoma and my author's group, whose support for this book through their praise has been invaluable.

Thank you Lisa Caskey, who was a patient, respectful and challenging sounding board in the early days of the NX framework, and to Tim Cooke, who helped chisel clarity from and add polish to my sometimes scattered thoughts.

To our clients, too numerous to mention, who have placed their trust in me and the LEXIGO brand over the years, your belief has been a driving force. You've continually pushed the boundaries in the application of translation and NX communication and engagement, elevating both our work and the industry at large.

And saving the best for last, a special mention to Jamila, my unwavering rock. From sleepless nights to in-depth NATIVE discussions, her support has been ceaseless. Together, we're blessed with raising three beautiful children, whom I thank for bringing endless joy and inspiration into our lives.

Index

A

A/B testing, 147, 201
accessibility, xxi, 91, 127, 134
active listening, 33
adaptability, 4, 50, 162, 178
advisory team. *See* NX Advisory Team
AIDA model, 111–112
ambassador team. *See* NX Ambassador Team
ANZ Bank, 108–110
Arabic language, xviii
audience, xxviii, 38, 44, 55–57, 95–96
audits, 135–136
Australia, luxury brands and, 10–11
authenticity, xxv, 9–12, 57, 59, 82, 83, 142

B

benefits, 160–161
biases, 32
brand awareness, 162, 183, 185

C

calls-to-action (CTAs), 160, 175
campaign kits, 161
case studies, 82
channels
    about, 102–103, 108

digital channels, 91, 107
traditional channels, 103–106
trust signals and, 91
Chevy Nova, 26
China, luxury brands and, 10–11
clarity, 141, 144, 145
C-level goals, 39
co-creation
about, 14–15, 128–129
5Cs Model, 140–146
four pillars of, 125–128
iteration and, 146, 148, 150
messaging, 136–138
sessions, 132, 133–136
testing, 146–148
cohesion, 142, 144
collaboration, 14, 119, 127, 134, 140
collaborative writing, 137
colours, xxi, 91, 96
communication
avoiding monocultural approach, 5, 62
channels, 72, 73
cultural context and, 56, 83
See also channels; language
community engagement, 127
community engagement levels, 184
competency, cultural, 31–33
connection, 142, 145
conscience, 142, 144, 145
consistency, 142
content engagement, 185
content marketing, 107
contingency planning, 192
conversion, 181–182
conversion rates, 184, 185–187
Coors, 25, 48
core team. *See* NX Core Team
COVID-19 pandemic, 1–3, 13, 149
credibility, 141–142, 144, 145, 169
Cricket Australia, 124–125
crisis management, 59, 63
cultural competency, 31–33
cultural dimensions theory, 65–68

cultural empathy, xiv,
    33–36
cultural factors, xx–xxi
cultural iceberg, 30–31,
    69–71, 78
cultural intelligence (CQ),
    27, 30
cultural representation,
    126
cultural sensitivity, 131, 169
culture
    cultural nuances, 11, 72, 96, 169
    heritage *vs.* home, 68
    See also cultural iceberg
customer acquisition
    costs, 184
customer engagement,
    183, 185
customer retention rates,
    184

D

data, 60–61, 64–68, 69–71,
    80–82, 83
demographics, 95–96, 98,
    192

design phase, 6, 20, 85–86
digital channels, 91, 107

E

education, 32, 34–35
email marketing, 107
emotions, 35
empathy, cultural, xiv,
    33–36
English language, xvii
ethical standards, 142–143
ethnographic studies, 81
evolving stage
    about, xxv, 16–17
    conversion metrics and, 181
    feedback, 193–197
    Kaizen, 179, 180–181
    reporting, 199–200

F

factors, cultural, xx–xxi
feedback, 137, 146–147, 153,
    170, 193–197
feedback loops, 163, 170,
    193

5Cs Model, 140–146

focus groups, 75–76

   See also, NX Voice Forums

fonts, 91

G

goals

   primary goals, 182, 184

   secondary goals, 183, 185

   strategy and, 94–95

Google Analytics, 64

go phase, 6, 20, 153–154, 155, 158, 183

grassroots distribution, 167–170

H

Hofstede's cultural dimensions theory, 65–68

HSBC Bank, 25, 48

hyper-localisation, xxv, 89

I

iceberg, cultural, 30–31, 69–71, 78

I.C.E. model, 30–36

   cultural competency, 31–33

   cultural empathy, xiv, 33–36

   cultural iceberg, 30–31, 69–71, 78

idea clustering, 137

inclusivity, xiv, xix, xxv, 14, 123, 126

   See also co-creation

individualism (IDV), 65–66

indulgence *vs.* restraint (IND), 67

interviews, 80–81

K

Kaizen, 179, 180–181

key performance indicators (KPIs), 172–173

KFC, 59

L

language
- Arabic language, xviii
- COVID-19 pandemic and, 2, 13
- dialects, xxi
- diversity of, xvii–xviii
- English language, xvii
- in-language vs. translated, 15
- pillar of inclusivity, 126–127

Language Service Providers (LSPs), 48

launch
- about, 16
- channels and, 165–167
- grassroots distribution, 167–170
- soft launch, 164

listening, 33, 73

lived experience, 77

localisation, xxv

long-term metrics, 183–185, 197–198

long-term orientation (LTO), 67

luxury brands, 10–11

M

masculinity (MAS), 66

McDonald's, 42–43

media, traditional, 103–106, 165–166

media kits, 161

messaging, 110–113, 136–138, 160–161

metrics
- long-term metrics, 183–185, 197–198
- mid-term metrics, 183, 184–185
- short-term metrics, 158, 165, 172–173, 183

mid-term metrics, 183, 184–185

mobile marketing, 107

mood boards, 139

N

native marketing
- benefits of, xxvii–xxxi
- factors for, xx–xxi
- in-language strategy, xxx
- linguistic and cultural context, 3

net promoter scores (NPS), 184
Nike, xiv, xxiii, 51–52
notability, xxv, 8–9, 25–27
NX Advisory Team, 44, 47–48
NX Ambassador Team, 44, 48–50, 62–63, 82, 131, 168, 190
NX Audiences, 44
  See also audience
NX Core Team, 44, 46–47, 63
NX Design, 118, 120
NX Network, 52–53
NX strategy
  audience landscape, 95–96
  channels, 102–110
  messaging, 110–113
  objectives, 94–95
  personas and, 97–102
  scoping out, 114–118
NX Voice Forums, 75–80, 83, 98, 147

O

objectives, 94–95, 132–133
one-to-one interviews, 80–81

P

personas, 97–102
perspectives, 35
podcasts, 105, 107
power distance index (PDI), 65
primary goals, 182, 184
prompting questions, 136

Q

qualitative data
  about, 60
  case studies, 82
  cultural iceberg and, 69–71, 83
  ethnographic studies, 81
  one-to-one interviews, 80–81
  sentiment analysis, 82
quantitative data, 60, 64–68, 83

questionnaires, 64, 193–194
questions, prompting, 136

R
radio stations, 106, 166
refinement. *See* evolving stage
reporting, 175–176, 190, 199–200
research
  cultural iceberg and, 69–71
  data and, 60–61, 64–68
  listening and, 73
  personas and, 98–99
  qualitative data, 60, 80–82
  quantitative data, 60, 64–68
return on investment (ROI), 184

S
SBS WorldWatch, 104
secondary goals, 183, 185
self-awareness, 32
sentiment analysis, 82, 116, 174, 185
sentiment consistency, 185
short-term metrics, 158, 165, 172–173, 183
social media analytics, 64, 117
social media platforms, 107
soft launch, 164
stakeholder maps, 130–131
stakeholders, 44, 47, 72, 130, 190, 191, 194
Starbucks, xxiv, 87–89
stereotypes, 32, 102, 113
strategy. *See* NX strategy
surveys, 64, 82, 147, 193–194
SWOT analysis, 116

T
tall poppy syndrome, 10
target audience. *See* audience
think phase, 6, 20, 23–24
traditional media, 103–106, 165–166
translation, 38–39, 42

translators, 48

transparency, 134–135, 141, 145

trust, xxv, xxviii–xxix, 12–13, 89, 90, 92, 118

trust signals, 12, 89–90, 91–93

U

uncertainty avoidance index (UAI), 66–67

user generated content (UGC), 170, 173

V

versatility, xxv, 16, 155–158, 162–163

Voice Forums. *See* NX Voice Forums

W

web analytics, 64

WhatsApp, 102, 165

word-of-mouth, 4, 20

About the Author

MARK SABA HAS SUCCESSFULLY built LEXIGO into the go-to brand for translation and native language communications and marketing, earning it a sterling reputation on a global scale. As the founder and CEO of LEXIGO, Mark has transformed a fledgling startup into an award-winning, global brand. LEXIGO is known for its cutting-edge translation technology and comprehensive services in localisation and in-language communication that spans 171 languages across 138 countries.

His forward-thinking approach has propelled the agency to the forefront of the industry, particularly through the strategic development of AI-driven, intelligent technologies that have fuelled the company's rapid growth since its inception in 2011.

In addition to steering LEXIGO, Mark is highly sought-after for advisory roles and his insights and contributions as a thought leader with specialised expertise in translation services, effective communication with audiences in their native languages, and emerging technologies. His career trajectory is a blend of management and marketing roles, with a deep focus on native language communication, technology and localisation—lending LEXIGO a refreshingly dynamic approach to product and service delivery that sets it apart in a crowded market.

Mark's distinct perspective is informed by his diverse professional roles and his enduring passion for technology, business and globalisation. Particularly interested in translation process automation, machine learning and his brainchild Native Experience Marketing, he constantly pushes the boundaries to realise LEXIGO's ever-evolving vision.

Residing in Melbourne, Australia and serving clients globally, Mark aspires to steer complex conversations, design better futures, and effectuate positive change, illuminating the path towards a more connected and inclusive world.

He offers practical, actionable insights—rooted in the *NATIVE* framework—that empower organisations to communicate confidently across cultural and linguistic barriers.

Connect or contact Mark by:

Email
- nx@lexigo.com

LinkedIn
- linkedin.com/in/mark-saba/

Visiting LEXIGO online
- lexigo.com/

About LEXIGO

LEXIGO IS AN AWARD-WINNING translation and native language communications agency that enables business, enterprise and government teams to communicate with confidence and boost in-language engagement across 171 languages.

With a commitment to delivering peer-reviewed, culturally-informed communication, LEXIGO harnesses the power of its proprietary cloud technology and advanced AI. This unique approach has earned LEXIGO recognition as one of Australia's most innovative companies in the Smart100 Index and a place among the Top 10 SMEs in the DELL Business Excellence Awards.

Founded in 2011 by Mark Saba, LEXIGO is a privately held company headquartered in Melbourne, Australia and operates globally.

About NX

LEXIGO® NX® IS A proprietary framework that incorporates best practice co-design methods and strategies to execute marketing campaigns that authentically reach, include and engage with audiences in their native language. Integrating the principles of co-creation, it goes deeper than traditional methods to create campaigns *by* communities *for* communities.

Meticulously developed for effective in-language, in-culture communication with audiences, NX is structured around three interconnected phases: THINK, DESIGN and GO. Each phase is crucial for establishing genuine, meaningful connections with these audiences in their native languages.

By employing this robust and dynamic framework, LEXIGO skillfully navigates complex linguistic and cultural environments while fostering authentic connections, enhancing trust and understanding with target audiences.

We help business, enterprise and government teams create impactful campaigns by delving into the cultural nuances of each community. Our strategic approach ensures that your message resonates on a deeper level and positively influences attitudes and behaviours. This leads to more meaningful engagement and prompts your audience to take action amplifying the effectiveness and reach of your campaigns.

- lexigo.com/nx
- linkedin.com/company/lexigo.com

Tune in for regular NX stories on The Native Experience podcast

- lexigo.com/podcast

Your enjoyment of this book is our top priority, and we encourage you to share your thoughts through a review on social media or your preferred book retailer's website. Remember to use #nxmarketing in your post.

At LEXIGO BOOKS, we aim to deliver content that embraces cultural diversity and offers insights into translation, culture, linguistics and in-language marketing and communication. To stay up-to-date with our latest releases, please email nx@lexigo.com and join our mailing list.

Bulk order inquiries

For bulk order inquiries, get in touch to explore opportunities for sharing this resource with your organisation or community.

lexigo.com/nx
linkedin.com/company/lexigo.com
nx@lexigo.com

www.ingramcontent.com/pod-product-compliance
Lightning Source LLC
Chambersburg PA
CBHW032335300426
44109CB00041B/965